3/19/16

Kathy,
in gratitude
for your story.
agape,
Braxton

D1508523

Becky
Van Ness

The Many Sides of Peace

The Many Sides of Peace

Christian Nonviolence, the Contemplative Life, and Sustainable Living

BRAYTON SHANLEY

RESOURCE *Publications* · Eugene, Oregon

THE MANY SIDES OF PEACE
Christian Nonviolence, the Contemplative Life and Sustainable Living

Copyright © 2013 Brayton Shanley. All rights reserved. Except for brief quotations in critical publications or reviews, no part of this book may be reproduced in any manner without prior written permission from the publisher. Write: Permissions, Wipf and Stock Publishers, 199 W. 8th Ave., Suite 3, Eugene, OR 97401.

Resource Publications
An Imprint of Wipf and Stock Publishers
199 W. 8th Ave., Suite 3
Eugene, OR 97401

www.wipfandstock.com

ISBN 13:978-1-62032-774-6

Manufactured in the U.S.A.

For Suzanne

Contents

Foreword

I'VE KNOWN SUZANNE AND Brayton Shanley for many years and admire their commitment to working for peace. What impresses me most is that they are among the very few who have understood the holistic concept of peace and how it can be achieved only by "becoming the change we wish to see in the world." (Mahatma Gandhi) Simplicity is the hallmark of their work and life. Detaching ourselves from the crushing influence of materialism is the first step towards transforming this world.

My grandfather, better known to the world as "Mahatma" Gandhi, believed that wars and physical violence ravage human societies everywhere because we have adopted a culture of violence which pervades every aspect of human life. There is violence in education; violence in religion; violence in pleasure; violence in commerce; violence in science; violence in language. In short, human societies everywhere on this globe are built on exploitation of human and natural resources. Most recently, in the middle of November, 2012, there were two fires in sweat shops in Bangladesh that consumed the lives of hundreds of impoverished men and women struggling to eke out a living in this world that holds profit to be more desirable than anything else. Many years ago my grandfather said: "If we worship Mammon we can never aspire to live a moral life." Clearly all corporations, multinational and others, work on the assumption that people are dispensable, profits are not. When human beings are treated as nothing more than a resource to be exploited by those who can, we are creating a major conflict that understandably evokes only anger, frustration and, eventually, violence.

"We must live what we want others to learn," my grandfather said, and I believe, Brayton Shanley has demonstrated this well throughout his life. *The Many Sides of Peace* is an excellent compilation of his experiences in living peace and sowing seeds of peace and not only deserves to be published but also widely circulated so that newer generations can understand that peace is not something one can wish for, it is something one needs to work for. There certainly are many sides to peace as there are many sides to violence—that take the form of physical as well as passive. We cannot afford to ignore the passive violence which is by far more insidious and which is the fuel that ignites physical violence. Brayton Shanley's *The Many Sides of Peace* shows us some of the important ways we need to work to achieve the goal of peace.

Peace can only be achieved when we stop oppressing each other, stop discriminating because of race, color, gender, religion, politics and economics and the countless other ways in which we compartmentalize human beings. It is only when we are able to create a human society that is based in love, understanding, respect and compassion that peace will become possible. Brayton and Suzanne Shanley have demonstrated this through their lives. May the fruits of their sacrifice be sweet.

Arun Gandhi
President
Gandhi Worldwide Education Institute
Waukonda, IL. USA

Acknowledgments

THE CONTENTS OF THIS book represent my lifetime of thought and experience. If I were to name the people who directly influenced this thought process, convictions, or writing, the list would be too lengthy here. To say that I have my own thoughts doesn't mean much other than yes, I am housed in my own individual body. On top of this body resides a mind and from the moment of birth this mind has been under the influence of hundreds and thousands of humans, philosophies, religions, animals; indeed all beings of the natural world. A book like this represents the mystical process of living my life and recording my truth. But it is singularly impossible to imagine anything completely "mine" or absolutely, newly created here. Ultimately therefore, I am gratefully beholden to all who helped convince me one way or the other, from my mother's love at birth to this present moment.

But one reality exists in the middle of this mystique of so called authorship. Other people inside and outside my extended Christian and interfaith communites have generously and skillfully come to my aid and helped me write this book better than I could have done alone. Daniel Berrigan SJ was one who has always endorsed and encouraged my writing, especially the essays that comprise this book. Mike True and David O'Brien insisted that I trust my story and suggested ways to break the code of "publishing." Fr. Emmanuel Charles McCarthy, the great teacher par excellence of Christian love that is nonviolence, spent many hours guiding the direction of the manuscript. Daniel Marshall, a stellar Catholic mind and Catholic Worker soul with great literary gifts gave selflessly to copy-editing and perfecting what I foolishly thought was the final draft. Arun Gandhi, grandson of the Mahatma, generously wrote such kind words of support for this book. Thanks to Liz McAlister for her life of prophecy and kind words. Tom Groome too, offered his endorsement and encouragement to this effort. Suzanne, my wife, is not like Tolstoy's wife Sophia, who just feverishly typed and copied the Count's words. Suzanne co-creates what I think and live, knows the utter importance of language, and has patiently hung in there for decades, guiding the rigors of my literary efforts and our writing together.

Words are a powerful force and "great books" of words can be a life's game changer for many of us. When I tell people I've written a book, they are excited and often request a copy—"when it's out." For all of you friends and acquaintances too numerous to name, who love "the word," you have given me the courage to complete this often arduous but thrilling task.

Introduction

THE MANY SIDES OF Peace—*Christian Nonviolence, The Contemplative Life and Sustainable Living* covers fifteen years of writing on the subject of Christian nonviolence and the central importance of the health of our environment. I have lived in a Christian Peace Community for the last thirty years while attempting to understand and practice the compelling ideas of gospel-centered nonviolent love. In 1982, my wife, Suzanne, and I, together with a core community of individuals and two families, launched the Agape Community, celebrating our 30th Anniversary as a community on our annual Francis Day celebration on our homestead in Hardwick, MA, in the fall of 2012.

In 1987, we embarked on an experiment of living sustainably with volunteers and community residents, by utilizing solar power, building a compost toilet, engaging in straw-bale construction, and driving "grease cars" that run on used vegetable oil—efforts that model a lifestyle that progressively eliminates dependence on fossil fuels. The chapter themes and insights contained in these essays flow from this experiment of living the many varieties of nonviolence in this ever-evolving ecological age.

Those who volunteer and live at the community are also students and teachers of nonviolent conflict resolution. Few would disagree that our world is in extremity as a direct result of the ongoing devastation of modern war and violent human conflict and the trillions that are spent annually by every nation to refine their weapons of conflict, relegating world peace and disarmament to only the dimmest hope. And our human extremity doesn't stop there. Over the last forty years, since the first Earth Day on April 1970, we as a human race, have awakened to yet another raw truth about ourselves—that as a result of the unhealthy food we eat, the way we use energy and consume our earth's resources, we have become the primary threat to the future of life on our planet.

We embarked on our community experiment at Agape, living out a vision of faith-inspired nonviolence and sustainable living. My writing evolves out of this experiment. It is an attempt to speak to the signs of these times, to encourage those who seek liberation from this ecological Armageddon by awakening to the possibility of morally and spiritually transformed lives.

These essays draw on the inspiration of the Christian religious tradition—the search for God, for the ultimate meaning that Jesus of Nazareth Himself reveals, with the conviction that a love that is nonviolent slows the dreadful suffering and hatred caused by fear. I try to write in such a way as to make gospel love not only an urgent necessity but also a real possibility in our economically unjust and politically violent world.

I write to evangelize a profound discovery in my life—a new and transforming knowledge of ecology is at our fingertips. We are in the midst of a transformational age, with cultures in a paradigmatic shift of lifestyle, a potentially enlightened age of social movements with thinkers who are uncovering the urgent truths of our times. Prophetic wisdom concerning life-saving technologies serves to slow descent into global destruction. Without such ideals, our efforts to seek peace in today's perilous world may end in devastation.

These essays describe a way of thinking for contemporary Christians—one that reaches across the spectrum of religions and cultures. At the Agape Community, we endeavor to live in the truth and example of Jesus Christ and to reach out past the divide of the world's religions to find a common nonviolent truth with courageous people of other faiths and lands.

Nonetheless, an academic reading of nonviolence and sustainable living is not enough. Instead, we must affect a conversion of heart and lifestyle, to transform an "at risk" human race, into one of peace. We will think differently, speak more compassionately, and be more spiritually prepared to return good for evil in conflict. A peaceful human race might achieve an historic watershed, a conscious choice to survive, as we grasp the moral necessity to live in peace with each other. Perhaps, in the process, we may learn to revere God's gift of the natural world that sustains our lives.

As the chapters dedicated to sustainable living attest, survival depends on a fundamental change, away from an essentially materialistic existence, toward a life-preserving simplicity. Such a seismic shift requires an inspired rationale, along with simple, practical steps following newly established scientific and sustainable methods. Coming out of our community experience, this book outlines a community's hope to be among the first sprouts of this transformational age, as we attempt to live a daily fidelity to an organic way of being.

We begin this journey by progressively eliminating all use of fossil fuels, replacing them with hard physical work, wind and solar power, along with the myriad alternatives that flood today's sustainable market. Such efforts create concrete, reverse directions which may mitigate the rush to oil wars and to stem the tide of global warming which threatens our future. Simultaneously, as a community, we embrace a vision of a more disarmed human race choosing the "narrow road" of war tax resistance.

As a couple, my wife Suzanne and I have chosen to live under taxable income, and thereby, to not cooperate with a taxation system that allocates over fifty percent of its federal budget to the military and to the human and earth devastation which follows. Such thinking accompanies a radically new experiment in living, what I believe is a spiritual manual for human/earth survival in this postmodern age. We need many such "manuals" which bolster the call in these urgent times for consecrated, sustainable narratives which create a design for a morally and spiritually bold and beautiful future.

SECTION I

Peace Is My Gift

1

The Many-Sidedness of Nonviolent Love

MANY OF US ADHERENTS of nonviolence fight an unusual battle over the word *nonviolence*. Because nonviolence is at the heart of our community belief system at Agape, we use the term frequently, leading to a challenge from some who are stymied by or resist this term. At our lectures and retreats, we often hear this remark: "I don't want to follow a belief that is defined by being 'not' something." Others say: "Nonviolent love is redundant. Of course love is not violent. Is there any such thing as violent love?" Furthermore, people tell us: "I don't see the word *nonviolence* in the Bible. So why is it so important?" Those who are familiar with the term nonviolence are often familiar with 20th Century social movements and noted nonviolent activists such as Gandhi or King. They understand nonviolence ultimately and perhaps narrowly, to mean civil disobedience and getting arrested.

Another frequent challenge to the philosophy: "Nonviolence means doing nothing under attack. You pacifists are too passive." When making such remarks, I wonder if people are actually rejecting the challenge of nonviolence and therefore discrediting the term as an easy way out of recognizing its truth. Perhaps the term nonviolence is fatally limited in most people's minds. I do, however, take these people and their challenges seriously, as I know for a fact, that most people who come to Agape attend our programs or join us at peace events and protests are genuine seekers of truth.

In our own imperfect way, we all search to know what is true. Because we want to embrace what is real, we seek to know the best way to live our lives and thus make possible the experience of what is both true and real for us. Almost desperately, we want to reject what is false and deluded. All of the World Religions and great philosophies assist us in pursuing this desire for a truth to know, to practice, and to live, while simultaneously rejecting what is illusory, fleeting, and partial. This journey of discovery, we imagine, will be of ultimate moral and spiritual benefit—an endeavor worthy of our life's time.

As it has come down through history, the term nonviolence, limited as it might be, is meant to represent such a search. If we pursue its origins, nonviolence is hybrid word, coined in English by Mohandas Karamchand Gandhi sometime in the early 20th Century. A common term for violence and its many variations has always existed, but before Gandhi, there was no term for what is *not* violent. The most universal, interfaith and cross-cultural way of getting at the meaning of that which is *not* violent is the term *love*, a word that compels our attention. Who would reject the miraculous effects of love as not true. What human, what forms of life on the planet don't need love? Gandhi believed this love that is nonviolent possesses "many-sidedness."

Yet, "love" also has too many self-centered meanings. A love that is nonviolent is ordered to an elevated place beyond just the things I "love." To Jesus and his Christian followers, a love that rejects all violence is "Agape," the "first love," the love of God as it is God's deepest nature to love. Creation is Agape, loved into existence for the purpose of creating love. For Hindus, Agape is called "Ahimsa," a non-injurious way of being rooted in being. For the Buddha, unconditional compassion requires living without harming all that lives.

Such unarmed love inspires one to "feed the enemy" (Romans 12:21), empowers followers to "turn the other cheek" (Matt 5:38) even in violent conflict, and moves us to forgive the difficult 70 x 7 times (Matt. 18:22). Agape is radically centered on the well-being of the other, the "person" as well as the "other" as represented by the earth's natural world. Because "Agape" as a Greek term was not widely known in the West outside of very limited Christian circles, and because love over time has been reduced to self-gratifying love, the concept of ultimate love needed a modifier. The term "nonviolent love" restored love to again mean Agape, the unconditional love of the Divine.

Engrafted onto love, nonviolence becomes a rich and varied reality which is complex and many-sided—a force, infinitely deep and inexhaustibly broad.

THE FIRST SIDE: GOD IS NONVIOLENT LOVE

WHILE TRAVELLING IN INDIA on a spiritual pilgrimage in the 1970's, newly interested in Buddhist and Yoga practices—I met a Buddhist monk. During our conversation, I confided my growing conviction that nonviolence spoke powerfully to me. I explained my college anti-war activism and the profound effect that American pacifists and conscientious objectors had on me, especially in my struggle to avoid being drafted into the military at age 19 during the Vietnam War. The formative influence of The Civil Rights Movement and Martin Luther King Jr., ultimately led me to India to explore the legacy of Mahatma Gandhi. The monk listened intently and eventually quietly commented: "If you are so interested in nonviolence, you should follow Jesus Christ." Offered to a cradle Catholic, this seed sown bore its fruit in the formation of a Christian peace community, The Agape Community, ten years later.

Agape, the Greek word for "the love of God," evolves into a nonviolent theology and religious philosophy. The early Christian theologians, Origen and Tertullian, living in the first centuries after Jesus, wrote of the uncompromising nonviolence of Jesus which anti-war followers later called pacifism. In the oldest spiritual tradition in Christianity, the New Testament, Jesus preaches, teaches and demonstrates love that is nonviolent.

James Fowler, Christian writer on the stages of faith development, considers a nonviolent faith to be the most mature expression of belief, calling it "Universalizing Faith," which knows no religious boundaries.[1]

As an ethical philosophy, nonviolence can be embraced as a nearly mathematical truth. In the Sermon on the Mount, Jesus teaches that violence only begets more intensified violence (Matt. 5:38–48). Or, as the Quakers say: "Nothing good can come of violence." To "violate" is to harm. Therefore, violence for any reason, never heals or truly reconciles national divisions which lead to war. Conversely, another equation balances these variables perfectly—love begets love that can only multiply love—even in the face of violent hostilities. This call of unarmed love, found throughout the inspired scripture of the East—Hinduism, Buddhism, and Taoism is epitomized by Lao Tzu, author of the Tao Te Ching who writes in Chapter 57: "The best soldier is not war-like. The best fighter shows no anger; they win with peace, not with war."

In the monotheistic Islam, forgiveness is epitomized by the Koran, as God speaks of the "merciful and compassionate one" calling the faithful to "council one another to be merciful." First and foremost, however, the ancients discovered nonviolence as endemic both to the search for God and the desire to know Truth.

THE SECOND SIDE: NOTICE THE FEAR THAT BEGINS IN THE MIND

Throughout Agape's thirty year history, community members have periodically ministered to the desperate poor in our town of Ware, in local prisons and on death row, Georgia. For ten years, we helped a local family, a mother, father, their six children and several out-of-wedlock grandchildren. The mentally and emotionally handicapped dad is functionally unemployable. The mom, marginally employable, frequently assisted us at Agape, cleaning before retreats and preparing food for those attending, for a livable wage donation and whatever we could offer as a bonus.

Dirt poor and itinerant, in and out of homelessness, occasionally living in a trailer on squatter's land with one or more of their sons and daughters at any given time, this family (two of whom were in an out of jail or running from some form of legal trouble) was virtually penniless. Any member of the family might call us while one or more of them were stranded at a bus depot and in need of emergency housing at Agape.

Several years ago, my wife, Suzanne found the eldest boy, Marvin, then 14, huddled in an alleyway, despairing over his family' s situation. He led us back to that family in Ware, which initiated our decade's long relationship. Over the years, we responded to one particular crisis—paying the electric bill that was usually many months in arrears. To raise funds, we knocked on church doors and begged for the hundreds of dollars they needed. Our parish priest gave immediate assistance. Yet, another local priest who lived down the street from this "notorious" family was reluctant to assist, confessing that "When I look into their eyes I feel afraid. But I realize I should be looking into their souls."

We have discovered that unconditional Agape love is what we believe in and desire to live out of, often places us in the company of so-called "dangerous people" who strike fear in all of us. This "love" is emotionally difficult and sometimes impossible to live.

Love that is nonviolent has a profound psychological dimension. John's first epistle states that "Perfect love casts out fear" (1 John 4). Great spiritual masters often say the primary psychological choice in the human condition is that of compassionate love over fear. Cicero uttered wisely, "We can neither love those we fear nor those that fear us."[2]

How much damage has been done to us, to others and to life on earth because of our fear-driven mindsets—fear of harm from the "other," the oppressor, the rampaging enemy, fear of scarcity, deprivation, starvation, fear of financial insecurity, and the most dreaded . . . fear of death, which no mortal can escape? Fear progressively convinces us that it is "me against the hostile and uncertain forces of the world." Conversely, the work of nonviolent love necessitates that we quiet our fear-conditioned psyches, trusting in the security of the Agape of God, love of others, especially the poor and desperate. In so doing, we can actually choose the goodness and superabundance of life—love over fear. The aggression of violence and its alienation from the potential for good, even in possibly threatening people, originates in a mind saturated to its depths by the many anxieties of being alive.

THE THIRD SIDE: ACTIVE PACIFISM

Since 2001, the U.S. military has been at war in Afghanistan, a costly venture, trillions spent yearly, with tens of thousands dead and wounded on both sides. A central calling of Agape's community mission has been to oppose all war, especially when conducted in our names. In March 2003, the U.S. added another war with the invasion of Iraq. As was the case with the invasion by U.S. forces in Kuwait in 1991, our community united with other peace communities in Massachusetts, traveling to Westover Air Force Base to voice our strong opposition to American military aggression.

Five Agape Community members joined with close friends from the Buddhist Peace Pagoda and The House of Peace, blocking the entrance to the base, momentarily and symbolically, bringing the force of opposition of nonviolent civil disobedience to this military juggernaut, the second largest supplier of war munitions in the country. As we looked up into the sky on that March day, we saw cargo plane after cargo plane relentlessly flying war material to the Middle East, on what was the third day of the effort to pound Baghdad into submission.

We believe that our faith and peace convictions need to be expressed publicly. We struggle imperfectly at such exposure in the public arena, hoping to act in the spirit of nonviolent peace, risking arrest in actions that we trust may create a moral crisis for those to whom we witness, bolstered by months of prayer and examination of conscience. From Gandhi through

Thoreau and down through the Civil Rights era, the urgent necessity of nonviolent love has been most memorably stated publicly by a prophetic and self-sacrificial statement: "No. Not in my name."

Nonviolence has a well-documented political history. We discover too easily human history drenched in the violence of war with an "enemy nation." What originated with the act of throwing a spear to kill or to drive back the enemy has today progressed to the production and use of aerial warfare such as drones and nuclear weapons.

In the face of continual worship of force, we attempt to locate the origin of the word *Pacifism*. Pacifism as a term emerges out of World War I, "the war to end all wars." A "pacifist" is one who rejects the violence of war unequivocally, sometimes out of a faith conviction and/or fidelity to conscience. For pacifists, no war is good or necessary. Pacifists refuse to fight, preferring to go to jail, suffer or die. They often vigorously resist war preparations, while steadfastly protesting wars in progress. Some Pacifists, as is the case with the co-founders at Agape, live under taxable income, one expression of refusal to pay war taxes. Why?

War harms and traumatizes, and those who wage it rely on a force incapable of revealing and healing the underlying differences that cause conflict to become violent. All wars, regardless of their "just reasons," leave lethal disagreements unresolved, thus paving the way for the next set of deadlier hostilities, emanating from increased division, self-righteousness and hatred of the other. A true nonviolent pacifist rejects war as an option, and instead calls for the embrace of truth in the midst of conflict. Pacifists choose the act of reconciliation and the severe and costly grace of forgiveness.

Aeschylus, the Greek tragedian, famously said as much: "*In war, truth is the first casualty.*" The disciple of nonviolence recognizes that the real revolution is the inner revolution. If we are curious about where wars begin, we only have to look within. "Where do the conflicts and disputes among you originate? Is it not your inner cravings that make war with your members?" (James 4:1) As nonviolent disciples, we do not seek to "vanquish the enemy" but to "vanquish the enmity." Unarmed love begins and endures by a miraculous change of our own hearts.

THE FOURTH SIDE: CONTEMPLATION THAT LEADS TO NONVIOLENT ACTION

The Chinese have a saying: "Sow a thought, reap an action. Sow an action, reap a habit." All our habits for good or ill come from our deepest impulses, the training and the conditioning of our minds. During our Agape presentations at various schools, parishes and peace groups, when I ask our audiences, "What weapon is the most lethal weapon," their response is typically not one we might expect—nuclear weapons. Invariably, most wisely answer, "The tongue."

Recognizing the truth of our interior violence, our daily community rhythm at Agape has emphasized a strong contemplative practice, as we seek to train our tongues. We invite people living with us to rise before dawn, meditate in silence, and engage their waking minds in *lectio divina*, a slow meditative reading of sacred texts. We gather for a communal morning prayer which centers on Hebrew scripture and Christian readings of the day.

The daily practice of silence, prayer, sacred reading and meditation aspires for the conversion of the "false self," conditioned by anxiety and aggression, to the "*new self*" which is cultivated by the discipline of "*new* habits of being" brought about by "*new* thoughts." The cultivation of such transformation, yields inevitably to a "new person" united with others similarly changed, creating a world, referred to by Peter Maurin, co-founder with Dorothy Day of the *Catholic Worker* "Where it is easier to be good."³

A love that is nonviolent is a day-to-day practice of putting on "the mind of Christ." We are made more patient and God-molded by a daily meditation on Holy Scripture. The apostle Paul instructs us that "Love is always patient and kind" (1Cor. 13), this love requiring the constant asceticism of inner work and self-scrutiny. As we leave our prayer mats and enter each day's demands using language to communicate, we concentrate on our use of words, inside and outside our community, as a nonviolent practice. We observe that the language we speak to each other in both tone and content is either a weapon that has the potential to harm or is the healing and reconciling balm of the peace of Jesus Christ.

As the inevitable conflicts of life arise, a primary need becomes apparent—the necessity to study and practice the art of nonviolent communication. Language that increases compassion joins empathy with training as we discipline ourselves to speak words that de-escalate violence and reject words that intensify it. A hopeful sign in today's culture is that the trained conflict mediator has begun to assume the stature of a peacemaker as such mediators skillfully keep anger-fueled conflict out of the courts of law where both sides in the dispute suffer and stay un-reconciled long after the legal decision is mandated by the courts.

THE FIFTH SIDE: RESISTING THE NEED TO BLAME AND PUNISH

Most of us have been raised on the threat of punishment. True nonviolence seeks a slow-to-anger sacrifice that avoids the knee jerk retaliation of "*lex talionis*," or "eye for eye" retaliation—most notably the revenge of punishment. For example, by rejecting use of the punishing hand toward children, we practice the highest form of self-control. Punishment, the threat to inflict pain so as to influence or control behavior, is just another form of adult to child violence.

Marriage and child rearing teach great lessons on peace. My wife Suzanne and I took vows as a married couple to live in community with the children we hoped God would bless us. In 1986, God sent us Teresa Ellen, through adoption. We raised Teresa in community with other children and adults who lived at Agape, many of whom carried the scars of the violence of their childhoods. We encourage those who come to Agape to work with mutual woundedness, being vigilant about signs of overt and covert violence in community life, while emphasizing the parental role of loving unconditionally.

We centered our parenting style on the seemingly impossible—to experiment with the difficult practice of punishment-free child rearing. Unlike anything we experienced growing up, this withholding of punishment became the ultimate test of our patience as parents. Nothing tests patience like raising children! What we meant by "punishment-free", is that we would not intentionally inflict physical or psychological pain. This restraint was challenged in the face of witnessing pain inflicted on Teresa by our seven-year-old foster child who lived with us for six months. However our children behaved, from mild unpleasantness to horrendously scary, blatant, in your face wrong doing, when conflict arose, we tried as parents to refrain from (1.) Raising our voices as threat (failing on various occasions) (2.) Threatening to hurt by immediate "consequences," such as withholding anything—normal pleasures, food, privileges, or seeing friends. We even tried not to inflict the standard "time out". For example, if communication during conflict remained too angry, we suggested that both sides needed to calm down, insisting that the quieting down occur in separate rooms. It always takes "two to tangle."

We learned early on in our parenting that blaming our children for their "bad behavior" as the sole reason for any problem and attempting to settle a "score" through immediate punishment only increased the child's feelings of powerless anger and injustice. Through the crucible of our mistakes, we learned that peaceful, honest, sensitive and truthful discussion, without harsh blame, slows down "bad behavior" and encourages "right behavior" in both the child and parent. Because we attempted not to threaten or inflict pain with words or hands, our daughter Teresa and her friends frequently responded with openness and honesty about their so-called "infractions."

As parents, it was important for Suzanne and me to communicate to Teresa that nothing she would say to us would ever warrant punishment. As a result, Teresa, now an adult, about to give birth to her own child, is quick to ask for forgiveness. Much quicker, I might add, than her parents will ever be. Persevering through the bad behavior of others is the work of patience, the word taken from the Latin *patio*—"to suffer." In this context, love is a suffering love. We bear inner pain of self-control by listening and therefore healing a child or an adult's pain and bitterness.

Our legal systems are based in a punishment ethic, exacting revenge on the wrongdoer. A nonviolent legal system would mediate differences without blame and punishment, choosing instead to see how most "criminals" are also victims of abuse and neglect. Innocent victims of violence need a true compassion and healing, having experienced terrible and unfair trauma, not the illusory false hope of "getting even" with the perpetrator, often masked as justice. In a nonviolent "legal system," so-called "offenders" are remanded to "penitentiaries," which, dating back to a Quaker practice of centuries ago, were places where "criminals" were counseled, healed, and enlightened with spiritual practice and trained in socially useful work.

Punishing young children only succeeds in making them angry. Punishing grown children, reared in this punitive mode, turns their anger toward antisocial. Sending a young adult from a tough childhood to prison to do harsh time for a crime keeps that person in bondage to a wounded, angry and violent past. It is we in our punitive society, who compulsively condemn, incarcerate and execute fellow human beings who are "imprisoned." In our quick instinct for the violent solution, we support courts of law, backed up by a fear-driven citizenry, who believe that they can prevent wrongdoing and protect society from the dangers of repetitive criminal behavior only by inflicting pain.

The reality of a high rate of criminal recidivism proves quite the opposite. Only love, compassion and mercy will heal our incarcerated sisters and brothers and us, setting all free from anger and the harmful behavior it breeds.

THE SIXTH SIDE: GOD'S EARTH IS ONE LOVE

By the mid-1980's, five years into living out the Agape Community in Brockton, Massachusetts, we experienced a strong call as a couple, to go "back to the land." Our major motivation was the ecological crisis bearing down on western and first-world societies for four decades. To slow this tide, we discerned as did others, a need to live simply, looking to hand-hewn ways, a more physically rigorous and low-technology daily life.

We thought that it might be time to learn how to build a house with wood milled from the land, to learn the ancient practice of growing our own food and harvesting wood to burn, through the often frigid New England winters, heating those in community. "Back to the land" meant returning to a profoundly human life, ultimately living with and learning from other forms of life, discovering what it means to be human in relationship to the animal world that surrounds us.

As a result of our community practice of vegetarianism and therapeutic fasting, we learned to heal ourselves from the excesses of the twentieth century—bad food and drink—and to become healthier through a daily intimacy with the wholesomeness of air, earth, fire, water and "other" animal life who share our land. Hard rural living, we found, is "organic." Organic we learned, is "lifeblood", and, in our experience, joining with the living, breathing, animated natural world. In our sacred endeavor to live non-injurious lives of compassion, we awoke to one unalterable truth—all life is one, and such oneness includes the non-human.

Throughout the 20th and 21st centuries, to be "nonviolent" basically only referred to humans learning to live without injuring or killing other humans. However, to love unconditionally, one must embrace life forms which exist in the complete absence of any political power, namely the natural world and its fragile ecosystems. Nonviolent peace activism stands in opposition to our society's plague of violence and cannot simply remain in the historically limited framework of anthropocentrism—that is, human beings mediating their conflicts on earth with regard only to other human beings.

When humans consider themselves and their intelligence to be the highest and most significant life form, their domination and sense of superiority over other life forms is another death-dealing oppression. We all know that environmental evidence shows that humans have not just done violence to each other; we have plundered the earth with over-consumption, deadly chemicals and use of non-sustainable energy.

In the 21st century, the human species is almost seven billion strong. Most of us live in or near centralized urban populations and rely heavily on fossil fuels. This over-reliance on fossil fuel and centralized urban services, coupled with a fear of scarcity has encouraged us to use the earth as a "thing," plundering the planet for our own survival or advantage. We over-produce, hoard and protect all the things we have convinced ourselves we need. To truly love is to experience all life as one, a sacred yet fragile web of being. To seek the truth of nonviolence, we cannot violate or coerce any living thing.

As a spiritual practice, we emulate St. Francis of Assisi, Patron Saint of Ecology, by seeking instead of the highest, the lowest place on earth. Francis shunned dominative power and violence, loving all in nature as sacred. In living closer to the earth's rhythms, we have found a lower place, and from that vantage point, we have begun to discover our rightful place with all earth's creatures and her ecosystems.

When we humans find our true place with created existence, we are celebrating the Divine Plan for all creation. This humble love restores us to our original goodness—to know by experience, the sacredness of life, protecting this sanctity with a love that safeguards all species—all flora and fauna.

FOLLOWING A NONVIOLENT HISTORY

Nonviolent love and its many sides have to be lived to be authentic. This living truth is also historical in that seekers since Jesus, and those who came before Him, have sacrificed greatly to live in this spirit. Practitioners of nonviolence have refused to participate in war and have suffered martyrdom as a consequence. Such was the fate of Austrian conscientious objector, Franz Jagerstatter, who rejected induction into Hitler's army.

Prophets and martyrs such as Martin Luther King Jr. have stood up to economic and racial oppression by living with the poor and refusing to support the drum beat to war. Dorothy Day and Mahatma Gandhi advocated loving oppressors into friends. Those who seek peace have cultivated, like the Buddha, the subtle beauty of compassion, through a fierce commitment to the introspection of mindfulness and meditation.

Wendell Berry and Thomas Berry are our modern day Isaiah's, prophets who not only confront us with injustice against powerless, poor people, but also injustice against the other "poor"—the oppressed earth under our feet. When we study and live this prophetic history, we begin to make it our own.

As handed down from the ancient Yogis and Buddhists, through the Hebrew Prophets, Sufis and the first Christian Communities, to the modern Quakers, seekers of peace recognize that authentic peace begins by re-making themselves and their communities. We spread peace daily by the way we live, the words we choose to speak, and the powerless outcasts with whom we choose to stand.

No one is born fearless. The ways of change from violent to nonviolent are not easily made. Therefore, we need to pray earnestly from the deepest part of our yearning hearts for the strength and courage to make this peace a reality. Our prayers will protect delicate currents of compassion while we progressively forsake the myriad forms of violence we have been conditioned to rely on, replacing them with the "many sides" of the peace that is nonviolent and sustainable.

2

How Are We to Live in This World?

THE BOOK OF ECCLESIASTES states that "There is nothing new under the sun." (Ec 2:11) Is it true that fundamentally nothing changes? Everywhere we look, we see ever-growing confusion, almost panic, about the direction of the world. Political candidates come and go, psychological theories emerge, and systems for economic change are waved at us. Yet, in the end, "this too is vanity and great injustice." (Ec. 2:22) "Vote for me, I stand for *change*" is the cry of modern politicians. Yet, history grinds on essentially, unchanged, and "What of all the laborious days and restless nights?" (Ec. 2:23) They seem for too many, to yield only unimaginable conflict and misery, decade after decade.

Because these systems and their ideologies result in so very little moral improvement, the wisdom of Ecclesiastes sounds intriguing as we are left bereft through political program after political program which only succeed in "chasing in the wind."(Ec. 1:18) Most of us are content to put faith in people who negotiate peace plans and spearhead revolutions of liberation, yet we seem incapable of understanding the depth of evil against which they struggle—a malicious cycle in which many who lead are often complicit.

Lasting peace and reconciliation between warring factions are so absent in our world because we seek them in economic plans, political schemes, and not in the power of truth that lies within. As a Christian, I need a clear intention to know the peace of Christ within me and to *be* that peace while involved in a world of dangerous uncertainties. Absent this inner revolution, we are left with the epidemic of violence all around us. Understanding this dynamic of violence and our relationship to it leads to a desire to be free of it, rather than to perpetuate it, or remain stuck "chasing after wind."

One of the engines that drives the conflicts of nationalism, class antagonism and racial strife, is acquisitiveness, or what Malcolm X called "dollarism." The real cause of strife is imprisonment in the psychological slavery to "things." In this embrace of materialism, to *be* is to *have*. We see this lack of freedom even in our comfort-loving church. The privilege of Western Christianity drains our life blood and courage. We compromise the gospel in the somnambulism of riches, routines and comfort zones.

The first Mennonites, while searching to reclaim the living power of simplicity and nonviolence, sought also to rediscover the core message of "primitive Christianity," to return to elemental roots of our Christian tradition, primarily in their refusal to fight in war. But by the 15th Century, Mennonites understood that the core message of the gospel had to be liberated from the corruption of time. This process of corruption began in the year 313 when the Roman Emperor Constantine made Christianity a legal religion in the Empire and culminated in 380 when Emperor Theodosius the First made Christianity the sole imperial religion of the Empire. From Constantine forward, Christians were no longer persecuted and, as a trade-off, they were enticed into the military. Political warfare and materialism married Christianity since that day.

CHOOSING POVERTY

Poverty that is voluntary may seem like an unusual way to peace. Choosing radical simplicity is a rigorous 1,000 mile journey we never fully complete, but must begin in our nonviolent effort to seek peace and pursue it step by step. In our daily struggle to simplify our lives, we at the Agape Community have realized that through obedience to Jesus, we discover that material goods are *not* the source of security. Authentic security is a mystery found in human courage, individual and shared reliance on God, and in "riches" that are found in Christian community grounded in relying on the common good, not merely individual good. Its mobility is consistently downward.

Living simply has more of the reputation of giving things up, rather than what it truly is—lightening things up. Missing in the negative connotation of "giving up" is the experience of "lightening." We give up what is unnecessary and lighten our heavy load of excess. Catherine Doherty, mystic, writer and founder of a Catholic Community, Madonna House in Ontario, Canada, writes on voluntary poverty: "I am interested in the poverty that makes us rich. I am interested in the poverty that makes us free."[4] Fewer things, less reliance on money, and more gumption for hard elemental work, free us to be a lean, rather than to be prisoners of expensive and relentlessly stressful technology and its "labor saving" easements. Conversely, good, hard, basic work using the hands possesses a dignity and humility that keeps us aware of essential needs and simple joys. When life is lived this way, a person becomes lighter and treads more lightly on the earth.

Living closer to the bone, managing with only the basics, preferring ingenuity and muscle require extra time, something we don't like to give up. For example, in our community, when a machine essential to the community malfunctions, we often attempt to first fix the problem ourselves. The freedom to use time, to live efficiently and practically is a voluntary choice. Unlike always relying on the paid professional, doing it yourself requires more of a person's patience, muscles, and intelligence—that is, more of his or her life's time. This has been especially true in learning (even in our fifties and sixties) to grow our own food, to cut wood for heat and to cook, build and repair our own buildings. Such choices challenge us to the limit, but the growth involved cultivates more skill than we ever dreamed of or thought we wanted. Not relying solely on cash for repair has also helped us to identify more with the poor and the marginalized who can't open the checkbook when hardship strikes.

Dealing directly with life moves us away from an unhealthy dependency on specialists. Newly skilled allies emerge. Case in point is that of the destitute family mentioned earlier who live in ongoing financial extremity in a neighboring town. Members of this family frequently assist our community in our own difficult times, as we reciprocate in theirs. They have loaned us tools which were essential for numerous homesteading tasks and have given us their old appliances when we needed them. Pitching in as chainsaw loggers, carpenters, and auto mechanics for our aged and expensive to repair autos, "Slim," the father of an often dislocated and homeless family, once plowed our 600-foot driveway with the oldest and poorest looking van I have ever seen. When the van broke down, he was the sole person who could repair this jerry-rigged vehicle.

By voluntarily living near the economic poverty level, we meet the involuntarily poor. From them we learn gratitude and the great lessons of perseverance. Catherine Doherty instructs us well: "Holy poverty should be a constant meditation. We must continually ask ourselves, 'How can I do without this? How can I substitute something less expensive?' For if we are slowly acquiring a reputation of having what is unaffordable to most people, how can we show the face of God to the poor?"[5]

"Simple" necessarily means "small." The energies we have begun to utilize are small-scale energies, for example, constructing buildings with our own hands, utilizing passive solar design and harvesting lumber, stone, and wood for heat from our homestead. A simpler life means being a "generalist," not a "specialist," and so that in a given week, my own responsibilities at Agape might move from lumberjack to parent to husband to carpenter, gardener, teacher, stone mason and bread laborer, then back to lumberjack.

Our attempt to live alternatively means that as husband and wife, and as co-founders of the community, Suzanne and I are freer to respond to the needs of others and the unpredictable urgencies that life constantly dishes out. We have spent most of our community life with little savings and no life insurance. For health insurance, those who live at the community rely on "free care." We qualified for free health care because we earn below the taxable income threshold. In this more simple way, we discover a person-centered path, rather than a money-centered one. We forgo the complications that go with earning a big enough salary to pay for all the necessary insurances and instead accept donations toward our ministry and community maintenance to make enough to afford the daily expenses of food, clothing and shelter for those who live with us. In addition, living under the taxable income level enables us *not* to pay for the continual wars our country wages.

Thoreau writes in *Walden,* "I went to the woods to live deliberately, to front only the essential facts of life."[6] These simple essentials allow us to peel away the false self, in order to get to the true self. To be lean in our choices reveals the true self visible, light and strong. As we in our community choose to live more on gifts, donations, Salvation Army clothing, furniture and house wares, the house décor becomes more down to earth! The less we desire to continually purchase, the more content we are with less, and the fewer distractions we have created by the constant urge to acquire. Freedom comes with fewer thoughts about money and as primary community efforts are dedicated to the service of others, offering hospitality, doing peace work, and resisting the forces of darkness and violence to the environment as they threaten our precious world.

POVERTY OF SILENCE

I am about to take a walk to our hermitage, located 400 feet behind Francis House, the community's main residence. Taking this walk reminds of me of the most neglected aspects of the spiritual and cultural life in North America—times of silence and leisure. We built this prayer hut separate from the main house. It calls us back to the need for a regular discipline of retreat -separating ourselves from the pull of work and accomplishment. This outbuilding is located out of view and earshot of the main house and sits behind an impressive rock ledge. As I climb, my aching back reminds me of the consequences of lifting heavy stone for building our hearth and the deep need for rest. I am going to fire up the wood stove now in preparation for a good friend who is coming to stay a day in the quiet.

Wendell Berry reminds us that since the industrial revolution, the operating metaphors for Western culture have been machines—inputs, computing, and accessing. Prior to industrialization, dominant symbols were organic, metaphors for living realities; i.e., Jesus is a "shepherd." Earth is a "mother." Animal care is "animal husbandry."[7] High technology threatens us with a rigid and sometimes heartless pragmatism, a "me first" rationalism that suffocates the earth-connected, the truly human and the mystique of the spiritual.

The most urgent spiritual need of this age is for a technologically-driven culture to re-awaken to the original beauty of the natural world and the life of the spirit within it. Taking time alone in the wilderness, to hand oneself over to a desert landscape, to the untamed mountains or to the serenity of the primitive woods begins to beckon us. "The wilderness will lead you to your heart where I will speak." (Hosea 2:16)

Entering the solitude of silence is simple, stripped down and elemental. People who request a day in the hermitage are looking to detox from the clatter of technology in our anxiety-driven and over stimulated age to find their true God and their true selves.

Solitude is dramatically discovered in the most dangerous extremity. Shortly before Alfred Delp, SJ was killed at Auschwitz, he wrote: "In history, testing includes both the departure, the journey into the desert to solitude and separation, and the return to the narrow streets of life. The desert . . . is a place of preparation, of waiting, of readiness, of listening for the word of commission. Woe to the era in which the voices calling in the wilderness have fallen silent, shouted down by the noise of the day, or prohibited, or drowned in the intoxication with progress, or restricted and quiet out of fear and cowardice."[8]

In gospel stories, we find images of people sharing pieces of their lives with Jesus. An occasional departure from these communal scenes occurs at times of extreme crises to which Jesus responds by retreating into the desert to pray and to cling to God alone. He returns from this desert silence to act; he acts decisively, and he acts in the spirit of a radical love. In extremity, Jesus presents us with a living model for action grounded in contemplative prayer and silence. With our reliance on words, the prayer of stillness is the simplest and most direct prayer. Entering a silent place unites the simplicity of lifestyle with a humble and transparent trust in God. Meister Eckhart goes to the essence of this mystery, proclaiming, "Nothing in all of creation is so like God as stillness."[9]

FRANCIS WAS POOR

We named our community house "Francis" with the expectation that this medieval saint would rub off on us as a community. Why this man and not the other of thousands of exemplary people down through all of religious history? The answer lies in the largeness of Francis, not grandiosity, but largeness. Although small in his humility, he possessed a powerful greatness of faith that speaks prophetically to these dire times.

On his deathbed near Assisi, almost blind and totally spent, Francis was widely revered as a saint who walked in an aura that reminded people most of Jesus. His wild, unshakeable faith gets under the skin of Christians then and now, stirring the heart as his story becomes a powerful sign of how we can become like Jesus. "With Pope Innocent III and Emperor Frederick II, Francis was one of the pre-eminent figures in medieval Europe . . . the Pope and the Emperor were born into their crimson and purple. Francis's career began in a shift of dirty old burlap."[10] His post-conversion life was a reproach to the assumption of career privilege. "He studied something we never learn in the boy scouts or with party affiliations, such as 'liberal,' in public schools or Christian homes—the science of social climbing . . . downward."[11] It would seem that any spiritual life in Christ, any spiritual tradition witnessing boldly in His name, must come to grips with wealth by looking squarely at how we as a people live economically, and the psychological and spiritual cost of such living. So stubbornly like Jesus, Francis has been called "The last Christian."[12]

Someone chided Francis to get a regular job, make the money he needed, and learn to enjoy possessing things. His response: "We don't possess anything because if we possessed things we would need laws and weapons to protect them."[13] Hence, the first rule of a Christian lifestyle: practice non-possessiveness. Add to that, a healthy non-possessive stewardship of the resources we truly need, because, as Francis warns: If we own more than we absolutely need, we must call in the state to protect these "possessions."

Voluntary material poverty is grounded in the desire to live more in solidarity with Jesus' teachings. With the prophetic words "Woe to you rich," (Luke 6:24) Jesus warns us about the forces of wealth that suffocate our true humanity; whereas poverty exalts: "Blessed are you poor."(Luke 6:21) Our present day Western world is layered with the "masks" of wealth, obscuring our true selves. Francis was a man without a mask.

Great moments in life, like great art, come out of trusting deep instincts. Francis's faith strikes us as utterly spontaneous—not the outcome of an obsessive compiling of abstract theology. My guess is that he would undoubtedly approve of most dimensions of Agape's main community house: wood heat, wood interiors, stone hearth, energy from the sun, passive solar windows with an expansive view of the land. We serve organic garden vegetables in the kitchen and live amidst furniture simple in style—donated décor.

I am not certain that Francis would approve of Agape's library, however, as he was deeply suspicious of books and did not own any. "Too many ideas," I can hear him muttering, "Jesus is found in simple, courageous, selfless action."

Such gospel conviction doesn't mean getting good at gathering facts, so much as getting us to *move* with what we already believe as true. Speaking truthfully and living precariously, out of our deepest instincts, we stay focused concretely on actions in our spiritual lives and not simply on the study of good religious ideas. Compulsive spiritual reading as a substitute for living truth can be another unnecessary possession.

History's great theologians are of one mind, that Jesus meant what he said in The Sermon on the Mount: "Don't worry about what you will wear, what you will eat." (Matt. 7:31) Many of these same theologians might argue that literal adherence to these teachings in our modern age is an anachronism. Nevertheless, scriptural relevance lies in the courage to discern the truth of what Jesus taught and lived "for our times". Our reality teaches us that the gospel maintains its wisdom, is unexpectedly relevant to "moderns," and is not time-bound. One can imagine Francis addressing the great Institutes of Christian Scholarship, saying: "Without pouring over your grand theories, you might have become Christian! Yes, preach the Gospel everyday but use words only if you absolutely have to!"

THE EARTH TEACHES US TO BE POOR

Why are we deaf to the language of the earth? No doubt in the medieval time of Francis, it was easier to live close to the land without the stress and clutter of technology and the damage already done to our 21st century modern environment. Many of us at Agape and the extended network of nonviolent communities struggle to be a lifestyle witness, which means for us, to speak to all life issues as one. As Christian pacifists, we oppose all taking of human life from abortion, to capital punishment, to war, euthanasia and destruction of the planet. Francis reminds us to add something to this sacred embrace of life—the Earth with its animals and plants.

A sense of the elemental that has been missing in Christianity, the seamless garment of life, requires the inclusion of the natural world. An ever-growing insight presses on the pro-life horizon: humans killing one another cannot be isolated from the destruction of larger earth ecosystems.

What the Christian life demands is that we see all life as a sacred web and all elements -animals, air, earth, fire and water are holy. A benign and Holy Presence informs all created life. What radical ecology people could benefit from seeing is that war and its ruinous toll of poisonous deadly preparations are primary polluters. Shouldn't all peacemakers become earth lovers? If we want to become simpler people of peace, we need to mimic the natural world and its creatures, not hoarding, over-consuming or contaminating with poisons—chemicals, pesticides and nuclear waste.

Voluntary poverty means moving away from the addictive over-use of high technology to enter the world of natural things from gluons to galaxies, learning a new language of the natural, feeling its sacred aura, communing with an existence that is stripped of compulsive excess. Finding our rightful place within nature and treading more lightly on Her returns us to the role of caretakers, of loving stewards of creation, and away from being a domineering force of excess and control.

The priorities of love, nonviolence, voluntary poverty and reverence for the earth are present in all religious traditions, although often buried under the popular culture of the day. These priorities reveal the fresh synthesis of a new spiritual age if we are to survive the life-threatening effects of global warming and catastrophic weather patterns that result as a by-product.

Can we liberate ourselves from the dreaded historical trap of thinking and believing as in Ecclesiastes that "There is nothing new under the sun?" If such liberation occurs, we will find an authentic change in human consciousness. The simplicity of doing will be grounded in the contemplation of loving truth and not just in the privileged ease of pushing the buttons of our modern society, convinced that we are truly living.

3

Divine Love

PEOPLE OF FAITH ARE in constant search of foundations, and for Christians, that foundation lies in the counsels of the New Testament. The most definitive picture we possess as Christians of the nature and identity of God is found in Jesus and the Gospels. The gospels possess a sense of mystery and are an inspiration to theologians who have sought to understand the Christian story in these four sacred books. No little urgency attaches to the questions of a contemporary theology, as renowned German theologian and priest Bernard Haring writes: "How blessed are the nonviolent, they shall inherit the earth. (Matthew 5:4) The question to be or not to be is now whether or not our planet earth will still have any inheritors and whether humankind will have any sustaining place on earth."[14]

We do not have the luxury of allowing our theology to become purely academic. Given the dangers of our time, either our theology will lead us to freedom from the dark forces hovering over us, or it will lead us nowhere, and we will continue to slide into cultural dysfunction and extinction. At the beginning of the 21st century, humanity—present, past and future—stands at this crossroad.

SUFFERING LOVE: ABSORBING VIOLENCE AND THE SERVANT OF YAHWEH

The self-understanding of Jesus is found in the "Servant of Yahweh" prophecy. For this reason, Deutero-Isaiah has special meaning for the Christian. In a principal way, these "Servant" passages lay out the characteristics of violence and suffering love that Jesus inherits. These radical standards, regarding violence and nonviolence, are then fulfilled, from Christ's baptism in the Jordan River, through His appearance after the Resurrection.

Historically, Christians have seen the foreshadowing of Jesus' suffering love and martyrdom through the events of these servant songs. "The Sermon on the Mount and Jesus' emphasis on nonviolence . . . cannot be fully understood without the preparation of the New Testament revelation through the Old Testament and particularly the songs of the Servant in Isaiah."[15]

The servant absorbs blows and violent abuse, yet refrains from returning blows, giving testimony by his endurance, not for his own sake, but for some Divine end. "He submitted to be struck down and did not open his mouth though he had done no violence and spoke no word of treachery." (Isaiah 53: 7–9) The unmerited suffering has a motive, a purpose, and a God.

Yahweh is able and willing to open the eyes of sinners and violent people to the fact that the violence done by evildoers will be overcome when they acknowledge that their wrongdoing is inhuman and sinful. God's dynamic suffering love, which Jesus saw as His mission and fulfillment, influences the oppressor as well as the oppressed. The servant doesn't ask why suffering is part of God's order but rather, the servant voluntarily accepts the role of being God's unique interpreter of this unarmed love, becoming both the lever of conversion for the oppressor and the force that heals the wounds of violence.

The servant fights the "war of patience" under pain and humiliation. "I did not hide my face from spitting and insult, but the Lord God stands by to help me, therefore an insult cannot wound me" (Isaiah 50:6–7). The servant, through his own helplessness and pain, transforms the meaning of all the suffering Israel has experienced by patiently bearing under violence and choosing to do so because God ordains allowance of the servant's trials and stands by the servant's side.

The essentials of nonviolent faith have always included Divine protection during the suffering of injustice. So highly personalized is this testimony that Isaiah may have been consciously appropriating the memory of a "martyr like Jeremiah and a sufferer like Job, now giving personal witness to the suffering human condition and how the sting of pain could be released and transformed."[16] Haring observes that "The Servant of Yahweh does not call for destruction and vindication. The servant brings healing. . . . He will not break a bruised reed nor snuff out a smoldering wick. He will neither rebuke nor wound (Isaiah 42:3–4)."[17] The battle of patience is fought with meekness as the ultimate weapon.

Such weapons were familiar to those in the Civil Rights Movement. In the heat of the struggle, Martin Luther King cried out: "To our most bitter opponents, we say, 'we shall match your capacity to inflict suffering by our capacity to endure suffering.'"[18] In this sacrament of voluntary suffering, we find ultimate fruit. "Through his wounds we are healed." (Isaiah 53:5) The victimizer experiences love through the quiet suffering of the victim.

Vernard Eller, Church of the Brethren biblical commentator, summarizes the servant's role in this fashion: "The Servant individual does what the Servant Israel should do. Since the mission of the Servant is Universal, those who shall walk on the roads of peace and nonviolence will form the 'New Israel.' The great prophecy of Deutero-Isaiah fulfilled in Jesus Christ assures us that the only hope for peace is in a faith that follows the ways of gentleness as of might. This composure under oppression opens the unredeemed to the might of love."[19]

Pointing to the power of the nonviolent tradition of martyrdom, the "sacrificed" person is raised up in sacred regard. Yahweh rejects violence as a means of establishing the reign of God, replacing it with a powerful, persevering love of nonviolent sacrifice. Isaiah's spirit doesn't end on the pages of Hebrew Scripture. He is the most frequently quoted Hebrew authority in the Gospels and his inspiration is found throughout the pages of the New Testament.

JESUS TEACHES AGAPE

Jesus doesn't come into the world to destroy the Mosaic Law, but to fulfill it, by intensifying its standards. In Exodus, murder is the wrongdoing of the wicked (20:13). In Matthew's gospel, even to be angry with a brother or sister is sinful, with Jesus commanding his followers to turn the other cheek and to love enemies, expressing in unambiguous language the unconditional love of God for God's people. Jesus commands us to love one another with the same standard. For the believing Christian, the Sermon on the Mount is the first time in the Judeo Christian story that God calls the faithful to love enemies.

An "eye for an eye" basis of justice is meant to regulate the degree of revenge of the wronged person. The penalty must equal the transgression—no greater. With Jesus, retributive justice is abrogated and we can no longer go to the law (Lev. 19:18) to condone even a just revenge. "You have heard that it was said an eye for an eye and a tooth for a tooth. But I say to you, do not resist one who is evil. But if anyone strikes you on the right cheek, turn then the other also." (Matthew 5: 38–39)

Jesus addresses the individual who has been wronged not in the abstract, but by a humbling injury. "Do not resist the one who is evil," means that the victim does not resist violence with the weapons of violence that the evildoer inflicts. Jesus speaks to the heart of the person bearing injustice by counseling victims to resist "justified" retaliation.

Despite the proverb, revenge is *not* sweet in the way of the nonviolent Jesus. This new teaching, in its rejection of "just revenge," is revolutionary for its time. Jesus' world was one under the law of retaliation, enforced by The Mosaic Law, the Code of Hammurabi, and Roman Law. "Resist not evil," taken from Greek *anti–histemi*, means to not resist "violent rebellion." The passage states that we do not fight oppression with violent revolution. A paraphrase of the ancient Chinese proverb sheds light: those that opt for revenge should dig two graves.

Jesus does not talk of converting the enemy, but rather He clearly defines how we can begin to change our own responses to insult. Injury to the left cheek means one is hit with the back of the right hand, clearly a humiliating gesture. To turn the cheek, one does not "escape" the violence, but rather forces the possibility of yet another injury. Nevertheless, the nonviolent person, so confident of his/her non-retaliatory position in the conflict, compels the adversary to see the full-faced dignity of the wronged person, as the left cheek is offered and made vulnerable.

The power of the nonviolent response implies the innocence of the victim receiving the blow. It is not so much a method as it is a piercing-through of prophetic insight. Into the heart of the moral problems of the injustice done in violence, turning the other cheek is the pinnacle of sacrifice, a response to violence that fundamentally requires the deepest courage of conviction.

Lanza del Vasto, a Christian disciple of Gandhi, writes of his understanding of the logic of non-retaliation: "Get your enemy to do twice as much harm as they intended. Why? Because the person who strikes you unjustly somehow knows that it is not just, or at least knows that in their inner depths. The spirit of justice hidden in these depths expects the blow to be returned. The oppressor needs a violent response. It enables them to keep hostilities going."[20]

Escalating hostilities created by the age-old pattern of the oppressor's violence and the victim's revenge is starved by the practice of nonviolent love by the oppressed. The back and forth of lethal hostilities de-escalates. Martin Luther King Jr. speaks of the efficacy of innocent suffering: "Nonviolence reaches the heart of the opponent; it exposes moral defenses and at the same time works on their conscience."[21] As in the scene of Jesus before Pilate, Pilate says, "Do you not know that I have the power to release you or to crucify you?" (Jn 19:10) There is never an absolute assurance that the violent injustice done to the oppressed, even when met with love, will alter a tragic outcome. Because enemy love is the Divine will, it is morally true, and can be trusted unequivocally and practiced even in life-threatening situations. We must leave its pragmatism up to God as the merciful Jesus does on the cross.

ENEMY LOVE—THE MOVEMENT FROM CONDITIONAL TO UNCONDITIONAL LOVE

"You have heard that it was said love your friends and hate your enemies, but I say love your enemies and pray for those who persecute you." (Matthew 5:43–44) This literary formula, love your friends hate your enemies was familiar in rabbinical circles in Jesus' time.

"You have heard that it was said" refers to the ancient Hebrew texts, but with Jesus, we don't have yet another text but a new teaching: "But *I* say." Jesus bases this teaching on his own authority. The teachings flow from a man recognized as the Messiah by his followers, who speaks in clear, unambiguous language, calling his disciples to his own standards in response.

George MacRae SJ, noted scripture scholar at Harvard Divinity School, in a lecture on Matthew's gospel stated that these words in Matthew 5:38–47 are "likely to have come directly from the mouth of Jesus, more or less, word for word." MacRae speculates that this is because "the Matthean church was a persecuted church, and not likely, given the fear of suffering and death, to possess such a heroic view of love or to express such a charitable attitude toward church oppressors."[22]

When our security is threatened, these teachings call us to the furthest limits of compassion. In light of this truth, we can never say "I will love the Nazis or the terrorists only if *they* change." We alter the dynamic of cruel oppression by first changing ourselves and then reaching the heart of the enemy by presenting ourselves as vulnerably nonviolent. Through the courage our faith offers, we voluntarily reject the illusion of the protection of retaliatory self-defense.

Love in Jesus' day was limited first to fellow Israelites, and then extended to resident aliens. But the grand commandment of universal love, now proclaimed by Jesus, includes everyone—gentiles, adversaries, and infidels. For Jesus, the "New Temple" is the human form. No longer is God's favor limited to a "chosen people," as all humanity now represents the "temple of the chosen." We are all God's people, even slaves.

In the Hebrew Scriptures, perpetual slavery was allowed if the slave was an outsider, not an Israelite (Lev. 25:35–46). By enlarging the "chosen" group to include *all* human beings, Jesus broke with the institution of slavery. To the Christian community, embracing Christ's teachings on nonviolent love is a spiritual evolution, as its members advance step by step in the development of the emerging moral equality of all people.

4

Jesus—The Nonviolent Messiah

THE WORD "FATHER" OCCURS seventeen times in the Sermon on the Mount, sufficient evidence that Christ is concerned with much more than an ethic. He is concerned with God, who he names "Abba," an intimate, personal God, a loving parent who loves without conditions, such love that we receive supremely in Christ. We have not earned such gratuitous love; likewise, we must consider all people embraced in that same heaven-bound love. God, by endowing us with the Holy Spirit, gives us the power to love. This first love, Agape, is a Divine reinforcement at the core of our new being.

This new love has many surprising qualities which instruct us in its ways, some of which are described in the passage itself. First, we must respond with more love than expected: "If someone would sue you or take your coat, give them your cloak as well." (Matthew 5:41) Second, don't be possessive. Unilateral generosity robs a situation of a further context of animosity and rivalry. Do the opposite of what is expected—return love for hatred.

The mysterious element of love is always a surprise. "Whoever shall compel you to go one mile, go with them two." (5:41) Jesus used extreme examples to make his point. Being compelled to "go one mile" usually meant being enlisted to do so by Roman soldiers. Love that embraces truth confronts the injustice of the oppressor, but does so without counter aggression. "Going the extra mile," on one hand, seems irrationally gentle in the presence of an occupying army, but by taking this step, the extra mile exposes the injustice of the forced march.

Many peace activists who follow the nonviolent Jesus have effectively struggled to "speak truth to power" by public protest, non-cooperation and civil disobedience. As in the Civil Rights Movement, these nonviolent actions challenge the oppression of the State and its laws, becoming a lever of conversion for powerful social change. Motives for this public and often confrontational witness must be purified of anger and self-righteousness so that these actions remind us of the Prophetic Jesus who risks his life by overturning the tables and "cleansing the Temple" of the desecration of "worldly commerce." (Jn. 2:13–22)

The directions gained from the mind of Christ do not suggest a careful weighing of the cost. The love command is not programmatic but prophetic, and seeks to make known the truth of God and to reveal how God loves. The Sermon on the Mount, together with the other New Testament Scriptures, makes abundantly clear that Jesus preaches an unarmed truth unambiguously, and that He teaches an unconditional, nonviolent love clearly, consistently, and without hesitation—even to His own personal detriment and death.

SIX CRISIS POINTS

When Jesus acts decisively, such actions are especially evident in crisis moments. Presented with danger, having little time to think, Jesus neither uses violence nor recommends its use. The first such situation occurs early in Matthew's gospel, the temptation in the desert. Satan offers Jesus all the Kingdoms of the world if only Jesus would bow down and worship him. Jesus replies, "Be gone Satan, for it is written: You shall worship the Lord your God and only him shall you serve." (Matt 4:8–10) Jesus rejects political power, the prestige of wealth and the violence that protects both. He is not a conqueror or a knight on horseback with the sword of deliverance in his hand. Satan says to Jesus: "There is no limit to what you could accomplish, for a price." Jesus could have limitless worldly power if He chooses allegiance to Satan and his means.

In an exquisite way, the New Testament gospels are designed to concentrate on the purity of good means, which is inextricably tied to good ends. The way of domination implies a right to render evil for evil, calling such evil righteous—that evil means can be justified by good ends. Jesus' way in the desert means that evil is not converted or made righteous by exacting an equivalent evil. Responding in kind multiplies evil. Ends justifying means has ruined the best of intentions and outcomes. If the means are righteous, the ends proceed from that same spirit.

Throughout history, the bane of all political leadership and statecraft is greed for wealth and power of those who run the nation state and the violence that protects that power. Such "worldly power" is at the heart of the temptation for Jesus. Although Jesus could imagine all nations under a sacred Israel in his Divine leadership, the coercive and money-driven means of gathering such power eventually corrupts his Divine ends.

The second critical point in the mosaic of the nonviolent witness of Jesus is the triumphant entry into Jerusalem (Matthew 21:1–10). Jesus rides into Jerusalem on an ass, fulfilling the messianic legend found in Zechariah 9:9 which predicted that the messiah would enter Jerusalem on an ass and summon his people to pay exultant homage. "Behold your king comes to you triumphant and victorious is he, humble and riding on ass. I will cut off the chariot from Ephraim and the War Horse from Jerusalem and he shall command peace to the nations." This kind of triumphant entry is the hallmark of humble love and nonviolent peace. But was it triumphant?

Certainly there were no trappings of royalty, but rather the image of a peasant riding on a borrowed beast—recalling to the people of Israel the prediction of Zechariah, a prophecy which lingered in the Jewish mind. People Israel knew exactly what Jesus symbolized—a peaceful, messianic figure who rejects political power and the entourage of privilege which protects it with violence. Jesus becomes the very symbol of the God of Peace, the perfect embodiment of a disarmed God. In becoming that symbol, he also preaches peace to the nations; that is, he commends the same disarmament to his followers.

The next crisis occurs in the Garden of Gethsemane. Jesus sees his crucified destiny unfolding before him as his disciples desert him, dropping off to sleep. In his anguish, he doesn't organize a violent revolution; he sweats blood. "And being in agony he prayed more earnestly and his sweat became like great drops of blood." (Luke 22:44) This is the choice we are to make in lieu of worldly power. The suffering of Jesus is the Messiah's grand design that invites his followers into a suffering community, one that refuses to meet life-threatening gestures with fear, a hateful word with more hatred, oppressive violence with counter-violence.

RETURN LOVE FOR HATRED

The nonviolence of Jesus endows his followers with an increased capacity for suffering love. Christians are to become a sacrificial community, a community of the cross. The cross is not a preference of tyranny to war. It is God's answer to both.

Martin Luther King Jr. confronted the murderous violence of the Ku Klux Klan with the courage of Christ: "Send your hooded perpetrators of violence into our communities at the midnight hour and beat us and leave us half dead and we shall still love you. But be assured that we will wear you down. And one day we shall win our freedom. But not only for ourselves. We shall so appeal to your heart and to your conscience that we will win you in the process."[23] In the pragmatism of nonviolence, evil is worn down by one's capacity to persevere under trial with suffering love.

Similarly, during his arrest, Jesus confronts the phenomenon of violence directly. In Luke, Jesus heals his enemy: "One of them struck the slave of the high priest and cuts off his right ear. But Jesus says, 'No more of this' and touches his ear and heals him." (Luke 22:50) Jesus loves his enemies by healing them; he turns the other cheek, thus healing the agents of his own death, illustrating the most extreme sacrifice—to love the aggressive, life-threatening enemy. This scene of absolute nonviolence is echoed by Paul's radical insight on enemy love: "If the enemy is hungry, feed them; if they are thirsty, give them drink; do not overcome evil with evil but overcome evil with good." (Romans 12:20)

An illusion of security exists in the possession of a sword, for example, in protecting our cherished loved ones. As one of the disciples "drew his sword and struck the slave of the high priest and cut off his ear," Jesus responds with: "Put your sword back into its place. Those that live by the sword will perish by the sword" (Matthew 26:51–52). Violence doesn't reconcile or offer insight into the true nature of the conflict. Something inherent in the violent relationship predictably escalates hostilities.

Warfare in ancient times was fought with spears and stones. Civilizations that followed continued to trust in the power of violence as protection from enemies. As nations throughout history continued to arm themselves, more refined techniques were employed—bow and arrow, the crossbow, and finally, gunpowder. In modern times, we have indiscriminate armaments—aerial bombing and missiles carrying nuclear weapons, and today, the electronic war of drones. The frenzy of weapons production is a part of a tragic history that flagrantly denies the warning of Jesus about the futility of violence.

VIOLENCE DESTROYS THE SELF

In 1948, after the assassination of Mahatma Gandhi, General Douglas MacArthur wrote the following tribute: "In the evolution of civilization, if it is to survive, all of humanity cannot fail eventually to adopt Gandhi's belief that the process of mass application of force to resolve contentious issues is fundamentally not only wrong, but contains within itself the germs of its own self-destruction."[24]

General MacArthur earns the right to condemn the use of force. How often had he looked out over the battlefield and witnessed its frustrated, futile outcome? MacArthur's experience told him that violence is incapable of achieving peace and can only produce more terrible wars and hopeless bloodshed. He states simply that at its root, the practice of violence is self-destructive. In a similar vein, Former death row inmate and close friend, Billy Neal Moore, describing his feelings after committing a murder said: "Something inside you dies when you take the life of another."

During his trial before Pilate, Jesus reveals how his disciples will live. "My kingship is not of this world. If my kingship was of this world, then my servants would fight that I might not be handed over to the Jews." (John 18:36) In this poignant exchange with Pilate, Jesus tells the Roman procurator that his kingdom, which was to be realized not in the hereafter, but now and on this earth, would not be ushered in by one final war to end all wars. His disciples were not to use the sword even to save the life of their Messiah.

Later in the dialogue, Jesus utters the statement that it is his destiny to "Bear witness to the Truth." (John 18:37) For this, he was born and given life. Pilate replies with a most human question: "What is truth?" (John 18:38) Truth is a precious factor to Christ, as he utters the word 88 times in the gospels. Jesus himself is "The way, the truth, and the life." (John 14:6) Because Pilate cannot enter into the reality of Jesus, he cannot see the truth that is standing before him; therefore, he has to ask the academic question. Scripture scholar John McKenzie, illuminating John's gospel, contends: "Truth is the divinely revealed reality of God manifested in the words and the person of Christ. The truth referred to in John's gospel is the truth Jesus speaks or witnesses. It is very probably this truth which is implied when

Christians are told to love, not in word or speech, but in deed and truth." (1 Jn 3:18) [25]

The truth for Jesus is love born of nonviolence. His truth is love. His love is pacific and is carried out with a new and nonviolent order of being. The spirit of this "messiah" is nonviolent; therefore, he sets it over and against "this world," the conventional world of power politics, which must use violence to achieve its ends.

Jesus dies because of the way he lives. On the cross, he loves where love is crucified. In Christ's crucifixion, we witness mercy belonging to the very essence of God's being. In Luke's gospel, the first words out of the mouth of Jesus after he is crucified are: "Father forgive them for they know not what they do."(Luke 23:34) His forgiveness is offered, not just to the soldiers who were obeying orders but also to the decision-makers, the Jewish leaders and their calculated rejection of Jesus.

Pope John Paul II wrote in his encyclical "On the Mercy of God" that "The church lives an authentic life when she professes and proclaims mercy, the most stupendous attribute of the Creator and Redeemer. Believing in the crucified Jesus means seeing the Lord, means believing that love is present in the world, a love more powerful than evil . . . believing in love means believing in mercy . . . it is as if it were love's second name."[26]

Emulating this mercy is at the heart of our commitment to nonviolence. The cross is the ultimate demonstration of the severe mercy of Jesus, the absolute stance that all enemies will be forgiven and that the God in Christ didn't come to carry out a "just revenge." Noted theologian and scholar Jurgen Moltmann states that "Jesus came to justify sinners by grace."[27]

Mercy is a love that heals the wounds of oppressive violence. Mercy is on the cross, demonstrating that God deals with enemies through sacrifice in which love finds its clearest expression. In our attempts to follow Jesus, John Howard Yoder, Mennonite writer and nonviolence advocate, contends that forgiving, nonviolent love is "the special test of whether the love we have is derived from and mirrors the love of God."[28]

In just about every phrase of the Gospel text, we find a nuance of the cross of nonviolent love. Jesus expressly calls his disciples to follow him on this cross life. We err if we think that the message of Jesus is to be admired alone and not emulated: "If any person will come after me, let them deny themselves and take up their cross and follow me."(Matthew 10:38)

In the four pillars of the New Testament gospels, the way of nonviolent love applies. Because Jesus preaches and practices merciful love, it is precisely this love that is to become the cornerstone of Christian life. We find a way to love one another as he has loved us. Heinrich Spaemann, the German theologian, postulates that "Jesus is nonviolent because God is nonviolent. God does not force; God shows trust; God sets free and guides to freedom. Nonviolence, just as much as poverty, belongs to the mystery of the Redeemer and redemption. The test is whether one shares in that mystery."[29]

5

Is Jesus Enough?

"I RESPECT THE NONVIOLENT position, but there comes a time when we need to use moral realism."[30] These are the words of Cardinal Bernard Law of Boston, from a speech he gave in Rome in November, 2001. The address came shortly after he chaired the committee which authored the U.S. Conference of Catholic Bishops' pastoral *Living with Faith and Hope after September 11th*, which lent support for the war then being waged in Afghanistan. Law's reasoning is that "moral realism" sanctions our nation's "legitimate use of force . . . to protect the common good against mass terrorism."[31] Given the present dangers, The Bishops' advice confirms force not only as an option, but as a duty.

In the debates and discussions on war and peace I have listened to over the years, I've noticed that all church "Just War" theorists are careful to state their sincere respect for the oldest spiritual tradition of the church— the theology and practice of gospel nonviolence, *but* . . . . In like manner, the Catholic Bishops' 1983 Pastoral calls pacifism "a powerful force for nonviolent human liberation around the world." *But* . . .

As one scans contemporary theology and New Testament interpretation, no voice of church authority disputes this historically and theologically accepted fact: Jesus is believed by his followers to be Divine in human form, and his words and deeds are consistently nonviolent. Because nonviolence has been a legitimate church teaching since the writings of Origen and Tertullian in the first centuries, and given the simple clarity of the New Testament itself, it would seem eminently fair and sensible to respect the nonviolent position.

If Jesus is "nonviolence par excellence,"[32] as Gandhi states, then it follows that the spirit of *this* Messiah and the spirit of *this* pacific nonviolence are one. What happens then if we take the word "nonviolence" from Cardinal Law's statement in Rome and replace it with the name "Jesus"? Now the statement reads: "I respect Jesus, but . . . ." What is the meaning of that statement? Could it be, "I respect Jesus, but I don't think his life or example are enough when all hell has broken loose?" Or . . . "Turning the other cheek works fine as long as no one ever has to do it." Or the more obvious dismissal . . . "Jesus didn't really mean what he said."

Does the logic of moral realism run like this? When our personal or national lives are under control and we are enjoying Pax Americana, and when we aren't being attacked and the economy is bullish, Jesus is enough. But, when violence breaks out and our lives are threatened, we need additional help. Now, the moral imperative is to be realistic—making it necessary to add or subtract from scriptural teachings of Jesus. When we have sufficiently altered the enemy-love command to more manageable standards, then we are free to advocate tanks, bombs, missiles, threats and non-negotiable demands to weaken the enemy, teach him (almost always "him") a lesson, neutralize his power and stabilize a conflict that is alarmingly life-threatening. Once we have accomplished some major killing of innocents (regretfully) and leveled the opposition, we can again re-open our New Testament and take its counsel. "We will be nonviolent after we get what we want."

The message of "moral realism" is that only airstrikes can, in fact, protect the "common good" against an enemy who is irredeemably evil and wishes us nothing but harm. Having achieved absolute control militarily, The Sermon on the Mount can be preached once again. When another "violation of the peace" occurs as with Saddam Hussein invading Kuwait in 1990 or Milosevic going into Kosovo in 1997, we are again required to put down the Gospel book and pick up the sword to protect the innocents.

In this "theology," Jesus is a convenient abstraction and Christianity is reduced to theories that are now debatable, and eventually alterable. In this thinking, the truths of the gospel aren't necessarily "living truths." You can't bet your life on them, but you must settle instead for an illusory security brought by deadly weapons and talk of killing. The demons possessing our "enemies" are chased away by our own demon-free, surgical strikes, smart bombs and now the push button war of drones.

Given the overwhelming support of The American Catholic Bishops for The War on Terrorism by endorsing a "legitimate" use of force by Catholic Just War Theory norms, is it possible that Jesus isn't enough even for our hierarchy and the institutional church? And yet, these are men who have vowed a life to Jesus. Could it be that many of those who lead the church, and many of those whom they lead, don't experience the resurrected Jesus as true and revelatory? When we experience Jesus as alive, powerfully relevant and Divine, Jesus is "enough." The experience of this faith enables us to stand up for the Gospel in spite of the cost. If Jesus is "the way, the truth and the life," (Jn 14:6) then act we must in this faith and in spite of our fear.

Martin Luther King, Jr. prophetically addresses this question of fear with civil rights workers just after he had received a death threat and in the wake of his home being bombed: "I heard the voice of Jesus saying 'still to fight on, stand up for righteousness, stand up for truth.'"[33] So, if the church's worldview and theology is compromised by a dreaded fear of unendurable suffering, profound humiliation and meaningless death, then our Church is not really "alive." Jesus is not alive within the church, and therefore, frankly, *Jesus is not enough.*

The power of Jesus falters when we Christians must face the sudden trauma of terrorist violence. The average Christian, under these circumstances, is left worshipping a dead body in a tomb. Our Messiah is reduced to the defeated one, lifeless, deceased. In settling for this hopeless God image, we forsake the central one—that of a God of Suffering Love on the Cross, the true God for these dangerous times. If we hold our belief "high" on this cross, we will have to endure Jesus only momentarily in the tomb, then we will triumphantly join him in the experience of Resurrection. Fear-rattling death horrors are now and forever conquered. But, if our faith is trapped with the entombed Jesus, He is a powerless, dethroned, and silenced Messiah.

If we live with our faith grounded in morally realistic "good violence" to defeat "evil violence," our icons, our crosses, our rituals celebrate an all-forgiving God-person who lived once, but no more. We cannot pin our hopes on Jesus to save us from the teeming violence of this world. Underneath our numbness and formal religion is a formidable angst. When our lives are threatened by terrorist attacks, we panic, and almost instantaneously, we surrender our allegiance to the desperation of "doing something", pinning our survival hopes on the military to "do something."

In justifying the bombing and invasion of Afghanistan, a woman religious said to me, "George Bush has to do something!" Does this translate to "The President of the United States has to protect our physical lives and all our earthly advantages?" If our faith in God necessitates bodily survival and at all costs, perfect maintenance of our wealth and privilege, then we have a lot to protect immediately, should we begin to lose "this war." All this protection, most Americans conclude, can be accomplished in only one way—massive bombing maybe even of civilians, men, women, and children, regrettable but inevitable.

Many Christians, who worship the "dead" Messiah and have left their ultimate concerns in this world to the armed protectors, may have grave worry if terrorists continue to strike. Spanish theologian Juan Mateos weighs in on this reality: "We either stand with the Crucified One or we stand with the crucifiers. There is no middle ground."[34] Most Christian leaders and parishioners I have queried, crave the middle ground, especially after September 11, 2001.

We don't want to be seen as people betraying Christ—rejecting his message and joining in mob crucifixion, nor do we want to risk standing with Him, stripped of the sword, empowered only by a truth that can be bloody and a cross that can be heavy. Instead, we opt to "worship" him while holding tightly to every earthly advantage, quick to condone the weapons that insure their protection.

To stand with the Crucified One is to divest ourselves of the economic privilege that makes the dynamic of war inevitable and to reject by word and deed the horrifying illusion that we can best survive the violence done to us by swift and heartless military retaliation, all the while assuming we are entirely innocent of any wrongdoing.

Bombs are thoroughly evil in themselves and completely incapable of resolving violent conflict or insuring any lasting physical safety or peace. After all the bombs have been dropped, the same reasons for war remain. New Testament warnings abound: "Evil simply can't drive out evil." (Rom. 12:21) The corollary teaching is: If we live by the sword (sooner or later) we will certainly die by the sword.

NONVIOLENCE AND STATECRAFT

In dialogue at Holy Cross College between adherents of the Just War Theory and nonviolence, Professor Ward Thomas, defending the Just War position offers a foundational truism: "Statecraft cannot be conducted by using nonviolence."[35] The implications of this statement run deep and wide in our society. Could the statement be rephrased? "Statecraft cannot be conducted by turning the other cheek or by returning good for evil. Affairs of state cannot function on mercy or compassion. Statecraft wouldn't survive employing love of enemy." I don't think that any one of the hundred people present at this debate would refute Professor Thomas's assumption that the federal government is not grounded in a truth which reflects self-sacrificing and compassionate love.

President Barack Obama, in accepting the 2009 Nobel Peace Prize, echoes this same position, stating that he has a profound respect for the lives and nonviolent legacies of Martin Luther King Jr. and Mahatma Gandhi, saying of himself, that I am "someone who stands here as a direct consequence of Dr. King's life work. I am a living testimony to the moral force of nonviolence." Then, President Obama inserts the classic disclaimer, "but, as head of state sworn to protect and defend my nation, I cannot be guided by (King's and Gandhi's) examples alone."[36] When the chips are down, statecraft as we know it plays by other rules, the lethal consequences of which always appear to escalate violent conflict. Obama risks another quote from King, the man he considers the moral North Star, yet again: "Violence never brings permanent peace. It solves no social problem. It merely creates new and more complicated ones."[37]

So then, what are the values that ground statecraft and help to order society and protect the so-called "common good?" Aren't the pillars of the State secured first by protecting our privileged economic interests, no matter how unjust? Can't we readily see corporate interests advanced by policies set by elected officials beholden to these interests? Scripture scholar John McKenzie clarifies this reality for the Christian. "What really determines the state to be unchristian is the basis of its ethics. The ethics of the state are the ethics of survival. States live in a moral jungle. Retaliation justifies anything. The supreme good of the state is that it continues to exist; no other good can be maintained if that good threatens survival."[38]

Statecraft's central values foster economic control where fewer people own more of the wealth both here in the U.S. and around the world with scant resources going to those in grave economic need. Don't our federal policies run on world-wide economic domination advanced by corporate globalization? Because U.S. corporations take their sizable cut first in any trading relationship and because Americans consume a disproportionate share of the world's goods and resources, economic injustice is endemic to U.S. economic policy.

Jacques Ellul saw that unjust economic systems are as violent as a rampaging army.[39] "I maintain that all kinds of violence are the same, the violence of the soldier who kills, the revolutionary who assassinates; it is true of economic violence—the violence of the privileged proprietor against the workers, of the 'haves' against the 'have nots;' the violence done through powerful corporations, which exploit the resources of a country that is unable to defend itself."[40]

Because so many Americans want more than they need, it is essential that the U.S. military be unmatched and goes largely unchallenged by opposing militaries around the world. Pope John Paul II labeled this system "savage capitalism." In his historic visit to Cuba in 1998, the Pope decried "neo-liberal capitalist systems that enrich the few on the backs of the poverty of many."[41] The U.S. machines of modern technology, that lead the global economy, run on the control of foreign oil. This fact necessitates the U.S. exerting a strong political and economic control within oil-rich countries, especially in the Middle East. We now see the symbiotic relationship between the desire to control and command wealth and the military force required throughout the world and the preliminary design for terrorist counter-violence, especially among the frustrated poor throughout Arab countries.

The World Religions all testify that killing innocent people is never morally acceptable, but could we be honest with ourselves and acknowledge that the violence of U.S. domination inevitably kills innocents, certainly spawning the desperate violence of terrorist revenge. So when the church says that the state has a duty to defend the common good with legitimate force, the question must be asked: Whose "common good" are we defending? Aren't we Christians submitting ourselves to a military operation, backing up a way of life that has made luxuries into needs; that is dangerously wearing down the planet's bio-systems; that will protect its interests by bombing everything that stands in its way—military foes and innocents, while trampling and poisoning our Mother Earth?

We are deluding ourselves into thinking that by pounding Afghanistan into submission and chasing down the Taliban with our surprise attacks, we will protect ourselves and our vital interests and rescue Americans from further terrorist attacks. The Afghan War that began in October 2001 has resulted in further social decline and slavish reliance on force within the fabric of our own society and has fostered fear and resentment of America around the globe. Trillions of tax dollars are wasted every year on military adventures that could be spent helping to meet desperate economic and medical needs throughout our own country and around the ravaged populations of the world.

The gospel truth is the reverse of this delusion. Nothing makes a nation less safe, long term, than its own reliance on unjust economic power and military domination. Because Jesus unbelted every soldier when he told Peter, "Put up the sword," (Luke 22:51) we are no longer in the dark. Massive military security at our airports and our Olympic Games only serves to illustrate how unsafe we truly are. Our gunfire and threats of killing adversaries will always ricochet. The hopeless cycle of Israel's retaliatory strikes against Palestinian suicide bombers should be enough proof of the teaching of Jesus—arm ourselves, dominate others, and we will die. Disarm and divest and we will live.

NONVIOLENCE AND THE SACRED

In the historical disagreement between justified violence and nonviolence, I never sense those who advocate "just wars" do so as a way of reverencing the sacredness of all life. Conversely, within the deepest wisdom of Christianity and throughout scripture of World Religions, I do sense a profound reverence for life in the various words that point to the spirit of nonviolence. *Ahimsa, agape, unarmed truth, compassion,* and *mercy* are all holy words and may be found in all foundation documents of the World Religions. They speak directly to the sacred and what is experienced as Divine. War, on the other hand, contradicts this "holy love" and fighting one could never be a sacred act. Arnold Toynbee captures this truth: "Love is the ultimate force that makes for the saving choice of life and good against the damning choice of death and evil."[42]

World politics rests on the adversarial belief in one country's moral superiority and economic advantage over another. Because we are convinced our side is on the right side of history, that our nation's propaganda is right, battle and adversarial conquest are inevitable, with one side seeking to gain supremacy over the other.

Governments find themselves adversaries over control of natural resources. The desperate claim of our political regimes is that when it comes to the earth's resources, scarcity exists. Put simply, there is not *enough*. Therefore, yet again, for many Christians, relying on Jesus alone is *not enough*. But for those Christians who believe in the living Jesus, for those who resolutely hold "the needs of the other, especially the enemy" not as a threat but as an opportunity to love, reconcile differences and live in peace, Jesus *will always be enough*. Doesn't this love ultimately reside in the heart and desires of all people and all cultures?

SECTION II

Peace of Mind

6

Where Is Your Mind?

LOOKING AT OUR WORLD, I often ask myself: Why are we humans so mired in conflict? Why is aggression the only realistic means of protection? What force is driving this view? Is there any way to find the source of this fear-driven thinking and unlock this tragic pattern?

As humans, at some point in our lives, we feel the overwhelming burden of our minds. The tens upon thousands of thoughts pour through our minds each day causing us to be at cross purposes with others, and with our true selves. These thoughts are the source point of our actions. The mind that churns them out has become a survival computer bank that is consumed with keeping life's dangers at bay. In this tireless vigilance to avoid harm, a war of inner conflict exists within every one of us.

The Buddha's central teaching is a doorway of insight: "Life is suffering." This inevitable and undeniable truth has a way of motivating human behavior and the experience of how we suffer begins to explain our tendency to protect ourselves by "fighting it out."

We all suffer, to be sure; yet, paradoxically, none of us wants to suffer. Add to this the fact that we also suffer from the fear of suffering and that we spend most of our time fleeing the threat of pain. This avoidance leads to more pain and reactive, protective violence that we believe will chase away our anguish.

Yet, it is certain that each day, every human will experience pain. We hurt. We become uneasy with ourselves. Should this anguish persist, it turns to anxiety that often leads to a low-grade aggression of words and actions in a frantic attempt to protect ourselves from distress. Our minds churn with escape fantasies, freeing us from our worst fear—being trapped in pain. How we seek to escape this predicament is telling.

As pain persists, our minds respond in over-drive. This is the embryonic moment for all inner conflict. Our minds start to construct reasons for our pain. To protect ourselves and our increasingly fragile egos, we stay within the self-justifying defense of "the victim" by blaming others for our suffering. We unload our complicity and wrongdoing by projecting it on others, on "them", while convincing ourselves of our blameless innocence.

Our pain, plus worrying about our pain, is then masked by the protective shell of anger. In this defensive state, even our well thought-out positions of who is right and who is wrong become defensive and self-deceptive. Without any self-awareness in these fear-filled moments, we begin our campaigns of harsh judgments and aggressive actions against the "guilty ones." But the anger we feel is always a secondary emotion, masking the primary emotion, a deeply complex mix of the fear of suffering and the reactive panic tendencies around the pain that is the root of our suffering.

There is no mistaking that Jesus teaches "fear not" at the most fear-laden moments in the gospels. He does so because of a revered New Testament truth: "Perfect love casts out fear." (1 John 4:18) The converse is the most lethal tragedy in the human condition: "Perfect fear casts out love." Self-protective anger inevitably yields to the pathological mindset that habitually creates enemies.

We "love" our enemies all right. That is, we need to have them. Because we cannot control or prevent our pain, life is therefore inevitably insecure; and furthermore, without a Divine source, we too often feel abandoned and alone in this unsafe world of suffering. Jesus has serious words for those locked in self-centered, fear-driven anger, warning that our anger will lead to "burning in the fiery pit." (Matt 5:22) Our thinking minds are habitually on hair trigger to survive (avoid death). Also, brain science informs us that our non-cognitive mammalian brains, namely, the brain stem, the diencephalon, the limbic system, are on extreme animal survival sensitivity. This physical firewall within human mammals becomes a fiery pit of destruction of self and others.

But if we practice becoming aware of the fear before our conditioned minds take over and harness it into angry self-justified aggression, we will discover a powerful truth about ourselves that might modify violence at its root. Awareness of the inner life is to notice our pain before the fear-conditioned mind reacts to pain with protective blame and retaliation.

I often overlook in my own mind, the self-control of watchfulness which I also notice missing in my peacemaker companions, nonviolent social activists. Too often, we social activists come across to those who watch us, as angry protestors projecting our unresolved inner frustration, bordering on ontological despair, onto political policies of our government and people who decide them, unjust though they may be. "We" are angry with "them." But a simple awareness of our anger releases the grip of revenge. The compassionate mind of Christ seeks not to search, find, invalidate, humiliate or kill our enemy which only multiplies enemies, but rather to understand the enmity with self-scrutiny, awareness and mercy for those we have made our enemies. Palden Gyatso, a Tibetan monk, spent twenty five years in a Chinese jail and when finally released, met with the Dalai Lama who asked Gyatso, "Was there any time during your incarceration when you were afraid?" Palden responded, "Yes. I was afraid I would lose compassion for my captors."[43]

Contemplative practice teaches us to guard the inner life with gentle watchfulness and good will follow. We "guard" by noticing, and such noticing is the foundation of day-to-day spiritual living. We don't need so much to study the world's problems, but first to study ourselves, "to dwell in the cell of self-knowledge" as St. Catherine of Siena advised.[44] This watchfulness begins with attending where our minds lead us. Why is this so crucial? As the mind is thinking all day, if we cooperate with everything it tells us, it may lead us right off a cliff—if we are not spiritually awake and vigilant.

CONDITIONING OUR MINDS

Why are we so fear-driven and inclined to protect ourselves with thoughts of aggression and anger? Quite literally, we all have been taught to be afraid. Since our first moments on earth, we have been consistently taught anger from our parents' impatience; from scenes of revenge on almost every plot line of almost every TV drama and Hollywood movie; from habitual viewing of football and other violent sports making violence the cultural norm; from the justifications for war and military violence from all our history books right up to the most current political crisis that makes violence appear necessary and heroic. This carefully instructed, life-long "curriculum" teaches us that violence will protect us, will resolve the conflict, will make us victors, and relieve our suffering.

George Gerbner, former dean of the Annenberg School at the University of Pennsylvania, made a 25-year study of the effects of TV and movie plot lines and scenarios of violence. He concluded: "Heavy viewers of TV suffer from the 'mean-world syndrome."[45] This can result in an unrealistic and morbid fear of the "world outside." Our minds are bathed in euphoric charges of retaliatory violence, our watchfulness weakened by carrying around thousands of hours of TV programs, media news and Hollywood movies.

Casualty records shows that a staggering 120 million people, the majority civilian, were killed in war throughout the 20th Century. What do these statistics say of the collective conditioning of the human mind? This cruel insanity of human history can be reduced to the simple maxim: Sow a fearful thought, reap a violent action. But it is not *them* and their war-mongering minds that cause wars. The real truth, free of our delusions is: We have met the enemy. It is our own fear conditioned and unexamined mind.

New Testament nonviolence begins with the teaching: "Hypocrite, take the plank out of your own eye; then you will be able to take the splinter out of your neighbor's eye." (Matt. 7:5) The plank is that huge, self-righteous blind spot. "I am the righteous one. You are the evil one. I am the innocent victim. You are the oppressor. I will deny my sins and call you the murderer."

Jesus suggests that my neighbor has a tiny splinter and I have a plank. My mind, conditioned by fear of pain and frightened and deluded by the 'mean world syndrome,' convinces me of my own innocence and the need to neutralize my adversary's ability to make me suffer. "They" no longer have a mere splinter in their eye, but now, viewed through the prism of my potential suffering, "they" are blinded by a plank.

Throughout the centuries of this bloody world history, what side in any conflict has not fought more fiercely by denying their own complicity in armed conflict while scape-goating their enemies as the villains? This conflict-escalating pattern is particularly evident in the Israel and Hezbollah rationales for war in Lebanon in 2007. Both blame the other for causing the war; both see themselves as innocent victims, and both conclude that fighting is absolutely necessary for their survival.

Meanwhile, U.S. President George W. Bush blames Hezbollah for being 100% of the problem. "They are the terrorists," he claims, in a classic case of self-righteous projection of his own warlike tendencies onto a group. And yes, Hezbollah is too often engaged in guerrilla warfare. But Bush's projection of his own wrongdoing onto "them," magically and instantly frees this "wrong-doer" from the burden of his mistaken decision of ongoing military intervention. Now we see all sides engaged in the deluded tricks of the mind that issue forth in the "justified" destruction of human beings.

Each side has convinced itself that it is the moral agent of "good" fighting against the evil ones. Combatants then justify the killing of innocents on all sides, which painfully but easily follows. All kinds of terrorism in history find their origins tucked away in the fear-filled minds of those who rationalize killing as necessary for "our" survival and security.

I recently read a humorous poke at Zen Buddhism: "It is 10 p.m. Do you know where your mind is?" In jest, this quip uncovers an important piece of reality: the majority of us have very little true awareness of where our minds really are at any time of day. Since we awoke this morning, our thoughts have been leading us around largely unchallenged. Many of these thoughts could be regarded as "trigger thoughts," a mind turned angry because of some annoyance. Our minds, like drunken monkeys, can go from anxious thought to aggressive thoughts, to irrelevant and then to absurd thoughts. Our speech and behavior too often follow that lead.

The awareness process begins with the simple commitment not to be convinced of everything our mind tells us. I am . . . and my thoughts . . . are. But I am *not* my thoughts and my thoughts are *not* me. To know ourselves is to observe ourselves throughout the day, becoming vigilant stewards of our behavior and emotional states. This awareness means being awake to our human existence within and around us without a constant self-protective bias. This faith is that a steady process of self-awareness will, as the Tibetan Buddhist Sogyal Rinpoche writes, bring the mind back home. "We don't know who we really are, or what aspects of ourselves we should identify with or believe in. So many contradictory voices, dictates, and feelings fight for control over our inner lives that we find ourselves scattered in all directions, leaving nobody at home. To train the mind is first to see directly and concretely how the mind functions, a knowledge that we derive from spiritual teachings. Then we use that understanding to tame the mind and work with it skillfully, to employ it to the fullest and most beneficial end."[46]Watch the mind with the dedication of a loving physician and this compassionate awareness will loosen the grip of protective anger that will "bring us home."

WHERE IS THE REAL HOMELAND SECURITY?

Jesus teaches the way home. "Enter the narrow gate, since the road to perdition is wide and spacious and many travel it. But it is a narrow gate and a hard road that leads to life and only a few find it." (Matt 7:13–14) Life is the creation of Divine Love. The experience of life is meant to lead us to our true home. But the way home is entered through a narrow gate which implies the difficulty of moving through a narrow, often harrowing place, that requires determination and skill. This journey will hurt on occasion. It will take time, and it might demand rigorous patience. Once the difficulty of making it through this restricted doorway into life is achieved, we are greeted with the challenge of a hard road.

The Jesus command to love is a universal call to look within, to examine our inner-most being. How will that introspection look on a daily basis? Like the narrow gate and the hard road that are a threat to comfort zones. How long will the journey require self-scrutiny and awareness? The answer: our entire lives. Overwhelmed, we may be tempted to numb ourselves with denial and to sleepwalk through life to avoid this rigorous road, a great and universal temptation.

The mind's conditioning includes a fear of struggle, as struggle can be experienced as pain, the pain we associate with need for inner change. So, the preference in the human condition is to try to avoid a difficult struggle and the vigilance required for looking within by choosing instead the wide, spacious, easy road where we perceive there to be little or no rigorous adversity. But, we still suffer in this life regardless of the road we choose. So, for what or whom are we willing to suffer? And why?

An immediate connection opens here with lives shaped by living in the US and our relying heavily on having things the way we want them and right now, achieving "happiness" through the illusory elimination of all suffering, *now.* We want to feel good, to enjoy our comforts, to live a happy life, preferring to take refuge in the ease of our privileges and entitlements. American life is the "good life" after all, the envy of the entire world. But oddly, we are pained throughout our lives by the fleeting nature of our comfort.

The "easy road" of the American popular culture assures us plenty of companionship as "many travel it." This crowd is what the early monastics called "the herd." Secure within the herd, we play by the rules; no boat-rocking, alternative thinking, no real introspection, no breaking away and walking against the grain. We are afforded a wide and spacious landscape. Any anxiety that gets in our way is mowed down by obedience to authority and the false reassurance of "us-them" morality. We are the innocent ones. Should anyone threaten "us" and our entitlements, we quickly mold "them" back into enemies. Our internal climate is a daily grooming and readiness for some form of war.

And where does Jesus say this "easy" road leads? To "ruin." If the hard road leads to life, then the easy road leads to death or worse, a steady spiritual demise. The truth of the Christ-centered life is that, admittedly, the world of violence is difficult to overcome in the name of life. But the first and most essential task in moving toward "life" is to move away from the narcotizing influence of the herd. If only a few find it, then finding safety within the masses numbs our desires for truth about our "life". The few who "find" comprise the biblical witness of ultimate hope—the "remnant."

St. John of the Cross warns us of the high stakes of rejecting habitually our comfort preference: "The truly spiritual person must seek in their actions what is unpleasant and disagreeable to their nature; otherwise, they will not destroy self love nor acquire the love of God."[47] Embedded in the hard road struggle that leads to life is the courage to embrace the challenge of asceticism and self-denial and the demands of transformation that always threaten our zones of comfort. Yet, the struggle of looking within leads to the greatest prize—the inner reassurance of a genuine Divine Love.

All spiritual disciplines aim at this sacred knowledge of the narrow path. The often "disagreeable" discipline of refining the inner-life of our thinking minds delays our violence-prone conditioning and lessens the possibility of committing unthinkable harm to others. Simple awareness of the mind transforms a sword into a flower, as we enter the blessed peace of new life.

7

The Nonviolent Word

A BAFFLING ZEN SAYING confounds: "The Way is beyond words." The mystery of what is true reality is strange, unutterable, and incomprehensible with words alone. Yet, to survive, practically speaking, humans must communicate with language. In day-to-day existence, our words express who we are to the world. They are a mirror to our minds. If the language we utter is not centered on the well-being of others, it can easily become a weapon. However, when we live consciously, centered in love, our words have the ability to reconcile like the healing touch of Christ. Yes, the contrariness of the Zen saying that we must sometimes go beyond the logic of language, suggests ultimate things are paradoxically beyond words. But the words we do speak can take us to the borders of the ultimate shores of heaven or to the precipice of hell.

My wife Suzanne and I plumbed the depths of language when we taught a six-month course for teachers and house parents at McAuley Nazareth Home for Boys in Leicester, Massachusetts. Founded by the Sisters of Mercy in 1901, Nazareth is a residential setting for twenty emotionally and sexually abused boys ages eight to fifteen-years-old. The school charter states a concern that the boys "pursuit of happiness often is hindered by their anger and aggression," a concern shared by the McAuley Nazareth staff who comprised the core of the program.

We listened to their first-hand accounts of how "anger sparks anger; aggression ignites aggression," leaving the adult caregivers, feeling continually pushed to absolute limits by their abused charges. Through their vulnerable sharing and frank disclosures, together we examined the use of language and its effects, especially when the boys and the caregivers are under great duress.

Throughout the program, the staff confided that the use of harsh and forceful words and actions with their wounded children did not serve to improve any of their relationships and were ineffective in helping students manage their own behavior. Threats and harsh discipline didn't create a more cooperative atmosphere in the school. Instead, their almost sole reliance on time-outs, various punishments, the teacher's glare and authoritarian methods were all stubbornly challenged through power struggles with the children.

Mired in frustrated and unreflective behavior patterns with our children, we adults retreat into our safe habits of coercive control. Consistent with what the Nazareth staff admitted as their own experience, adults can become locked in battles with children that they cannot win. We all agreed that many adults simply never think about the serious effects our threatening words and ultimatums have on children. To take ownership of our words, especially with children who have experienced trauma, is to begin to observe our own internal violence.

Psychiatrist Leonard Shengold who has worked with patients abused in childhood writes in his seminal book *Soul Murder Revisited* that childhood abuse leaves profound marks on the psyche. "In the disturbed child's mind, fantasy and reality are difficult to disentangle." He emphasizes the awful effects of "overstimulation, attendant in all abuse, where the trauma is so overwhelming, and such a sensory overload, that the mental apparatus is flooded with feeling. This sensory overload may lead to erotic excitement or rage so unbearable that the child becomes numb and without feeling. Like those who often become brutal through suffering brutality, the abused child is likely to grow up into an abusive adult."[48] The adult teachers and caregivers at Nazareth were dealing on a daily basis with the most demanding cases of these abused children.

In reality, most children hear the abuse of continual threats throughout their childhoods. A powerless class, these youth become filled with rage, fueled by day-in and day-out yelling of ultimatums, justified by the thinking among those in authority that youthful behavior has to be controlled—especially "bad" behavior. So, we order, warn, ridicule and punish, even the most wounded children.

Those who work with youth are often too proud or too set in their imposing attitudes to admit that they too feel powerless and afraid in the presence of the difficult and angry child. In a desperate attempt to bend children to their will, adults impose ultimatums as solutions. Children voicing their deepest needs and exercising their freedom to choose are completely absent in many contentious interactions. As the Nazareth staff in this nonviolent communication course kept reminding us, "Our children untiringly resist being told what to do."

When children have lost trust in adults or sense they are not being heard, they use verbal attack patterns, a hostile gesture or words designed to create angry reactions in the adult, thus gaining power through desired attention. This assault creates a hostility loop which is then escalated by the adults' threats and punishing gestures. Unable to see the child's desperate pleas to be heard, to command attention, adults often simply respond through the controlling impulse of threat, creating a conflict of needs often resulting in the child's experience of humiliation.

Children need space to be truly heard and appreciated. Adults need respite from the mounting stress of patterned and repetitive oppositional behavior that easily overwhelms other children present and the adults in authority. Yet, when tensions mount, blame, physical restraint or worse are employed to isolate an out of control child. This "stubborn child" is often yelled at, grabbed, sent to "time-out" or detention with the result that the underlying needs of both child and caregiver are never understood or honestly shared.

The great tragedy in this interplay is that the native compassion of adults, especially for the "vulnerable child," is compromised. In the face of a child's apparent unmanageability, threatened adults tend to recoil in anger, relying on force for their authority. Compound this reaction with mounting frustration and guilt over these retaliatory reactions on both sides, and we have a no-win situation. Most parents and teachers of youth employ some patterns of inflicting pain, often justified as a constructive use of "consequences for their behavior." Adults who repress significant guilt for these hardball methods continue to compound the pattern, often needing to escalate punishment and consequences as situations become more unmanageable. Many abused children experience extreme guilt and self-loathing, which is exacerbated by escalating conflict with an adult. If we continue to use force to resolve conflicts, we will forfeit our influence on children. They will, quite literally, stop listening to us.

PUNISHMENT IS VIOLENCE

James Gilligan has listened to life stories from male prison inmates for 25 years as a psychiatrist at Bridgewater State Hospital for the criminally insane in Massachusetts. He shares valuable insights in his book, *Violence: Reflections on a National Epidemic* through story after story from inmates who convinced him that the more harshly we punish children, the more violent they become. For Gilligan, punishment itself, the legally sanctioned inflicting of pain[49] so as to humiliate or control behaviors is a form of violence and inevitably, becomes a way of encouraging revenge in our children. Gilligan insists that "Punishment stimulates violence; punishment causes it. The more punitive our society has become, the higher our rate of violence both criminal and noncriminal has become."[50]

Male inmates he counseled acted out of rage that stemmed from the humiliation of punishing shame that they experienced as children. "Punishment increases their feelings of shame and simultaneously decreases their capacities for feelings of love for others and of guilt toward others."[51] By the time these young men have been convicted of serious crimes, they have often endured long childhoods of humiliation. Sr. Carol, an administrator at McAuley Nazareth shared with us the sad fact that some of their students end up doing long prison sentences as adults. The Sisters of Mercy often spoke about the dream of a fourteen-year-old boy in their care, to end up in maximum-security prison which he viewed as a great badge of macho courage after his childhood of rage and hurt.

Teachers and administrators at Nazareth expressed the feeling that their children lacked the normal human pangs of conscience, and a sense of moral right and wrong that "everyday" children generally have. Their students had experienced continual abuse as young children. Therefore, as Gilligan suggests, such abuse had neutralized appropriate capacities for conscience and healthy feelings of guilt in favor of more angry and aggressive behavior. Both teachers and house parents had to look seriously at how their "disciplining" might have been reinforcing the Nazareth boys' previous experiences of shaming.[52]

What we in the program were learning was that in legal and social realms, punishment is violence and that it encourages counter-violence. Taken from the Latin word, "poena" meaning pain, to inflict suffering in an effort to improve behavior for any reasons only increases the recipient's sense of powerlessness, leaving resistance as their sole recourse. We adults must become aware of how our allegiance to coercion wielded by those in authority only serves to exercise our own wounded frustration that often originates from our own experiences of powerlessness as children.

Children have no choice but to absorb their surroundings, including often dangerously stressed and controlling parents, the punitive world of school and peers who bully them. Most of us have no other data and virtually no other modeling but that of "fight to win." We assume, for example, that anti-social violence can only be subdued by imposing our own "lesson learning violence."

When we bow to this lie of "redemptive" violence, that *our* violence will end violence, we profess our deepest trust and our real faith in every crisis and conflict. Authority figures feel morally compelled to punish obstinate "underlings" who challenge or threaten their authority. The necessity to inflict suffering that will somehow redeem a conflict from further violence knows no boundaries culturally or politically. Such views of punishment simply operate at all levels of human culture from child rearing outward to all schools and social institutions, to politics and governance at every level.

Into history comes Jesus of Nazareth and the telling of a different story. At its heart, His is a story contrary to our conditioned thinking on moral and social consequences of "bad behavior." Jesus asks us to consider redemption and posits that only good conquers violence, and that we can convert the violent ones by responding only in love.

Jesus' counter narrative relies on the premise that "they" will change only if "I" change. The miracle of this nonviolent practice is that the responsibility for the quality of human interaction falls on *me. I am the listener. I am the consoler. I absorb and acknowledge the pain of the enemy. I grant freedom from violence to my adversaries so that they might freely choose to right their course toward the good of all, trusting that this is their deepest desire.*

The nonviolent perspective is that *I* own the problem which demands that I look seriously at the spirit of *my* language. The title of our course at McCauley Nazareth could easily have been titled, "How can I talk so that children will listen?" Or even the reverse, "How can I listen, so that children will talk?" Very exciting strides have taken place in the last twenty years regarding mediation, nonviolent communication and conflict resolution. Practice of nonviolent communication at Nazareth began to shed light on a gnawing sense of the staff that coercive disciplinary practices don't change bad behavior for the good in any lasting sense. One extremely conscientious teacher, in her unfaltering attempts to deal with the most difficult child at

McAuley Nazareth during the time we were there, when asked honestly if all of the "time-outs" changed this child's behavior for the good, confided, "No."

Frequent role-plays among the adult participants were most intriguing and instructive for all of us as we assumed the identities of adult and child interchangeably. We felt the rage of the children in our own beings. House parents, for example, were able to identify more with teachers and the teachers with administrators, all gaining more sympathy with the overwhelming struggle of the children themselves.

Many hilarious moments ensued as we put ourselves in various roles, with much laughter and bantering, all serving the purpose of looking at ourselves. With the habit of punishment as a controlling mechanism, the staff began to realize that they were preoccupied with maintaining punishment protocols, rather than with exploring "win-win solutions," which created more positive disciplines and dialogue. Eventually, sometimes reluctantly, we came to the conclusion that no child should be punished or humiliated to keep the peace.

Jesus is clear in handling serious conflict. He rejects violence, embracing the hated Samaritans as friends and shows his objection to fighting evil with evil (Luke 13:1–3). If we take his lead, we are not likely to deal with any contentious child with power talk or the continual threat of pain, but we will engage them with our compassionate responses. Direct engagement with nonviolent words is always best.

DE-ESCALATING CONFLICT WITH DIALOGUE

An adult-initiated discussion about the origin of animosities with the difficult child respects the dignity of the child, so that both parties are allowed to express their needs, not their positions or ultimatums. Expressing needs honestly opens a sympathetic heart in both parties. Positions are like a fortress which we think will protect us but, in reality, only serve to prevent the discovery of resolutions to a conflict. Expressing our needs evokes compassion. Our "positions" evoke resistance and opposition.

Adults proceed with a handicap in that men and women with power and authority are so conditioned by the advantages of their authority that they will be tempted to stay "in charge," reluctant to give up power by truly listening to the needs of the child. The fact is that children, especially abused children, have experienced environments where they are never heard. For them finally to experience someone listening to their pain and confusion immediately begins unlocking the hostility loop that hopelessly and tightly grips the conflict.

Imagine what would happen if negotiating parties communicated real existential needs, not retaliatory strikes—genuine honesty and not rigid positions, refusing to abdicate a listening dialogue for explosive words. Most adults in conflict with children shake with self-righteous anger largely because they feel humiliated when their authority is threatened. Children feel powerless and in perpetual fear of punishment. In their frustration, those holding the power get to frame the argument. They are convinced that the "other" needs to change. The "other" is the problem. The internal refrain of the nonviolent practitioner is the contrary. A true peacemaker asks in the heat of painful "warfare" whether with an abused child or any adversary: "What is it in me that needs to change? How can I identify with my adversary's suffering? Why are they so angry?"

The real truth in a disagreement comes from deep within a person. Dr. Thomas Gordon, well known for his Parent Effectiveness Training books and workshops writes profoundly on adult-child conflict.[53] The heart of his technique consists in getting the blame word, "you," out of our active vocabulary. *You did this. You are wrong. You are the closest thing to Adolf Hitler. You should know better.* These "you" utterances are self-righteous projections because we make the other party so obviously at fault. In the meantime, the accusing party feels utterly innocent of any significant blame.

Gordon invites us instead, to communicate an "I" message. If an adult or child is full of stress and fear and my behavior is frustrating them, the nonviolent approach is first to own the problem, using "I" messages. I share my state of being. Because I am rejecting bullying or domination in the process, I have entered two important conflict de-escalating realms: (1.) I have broken any cycle of retaliatory hostility, and (2.) I have started a process of listening to myself and to the one with whom I am in conflict.

Through active listening, I invite the adversary out of his/her chosen freedom to honest dialogue beginning with the words: "I feel (an honest emotion about how I felt about a negative interaction) . . . when you (point to a specific comment or incident of concern) . . . because (my reasons for thinking that the behavior or comment is a problem) . . . I need you to (offer a reasonable practical suggestion that alters the negative pattern) . . . " When speaking to a young person about his/her behavior we could sound like this; "*I feel* frustrated *when you* talk out of turn in class *because* I am trying to teach you something that I think is important. *I need you to* raise your hand to be recognized before you speak in the class." In this process, both adult and child have a non-blaming reference point and a practical solution suggested when communication breaks down.

Then, out of this new exploration, each side enters into a dialogue that now manages conflict more successfully, out of mutual understanding of personal needs. It may seem easier for the adult to remain adversarial due to the power advantage. It takes courage to resist that advantage, to face our own pain and that of the child and then to engage with vulnerability and trust. If we give it a chance, we will quickly conclude that nonviolent communication is the only valid method to change the behavior of all parties in a more lasting and peace-filled way.

Sr. Carol, an administrator at McAuley Nazareth carried the "I" messages and a list of hints for de-escalating conflict on a piece of paper and consulted them daily. She was a testimony to the efficacy of the program, with all of its points of vulnerability and painful self-assessment. At the program's conclusion, we all felt what the administration confirmed in their final written evaluations: "We are more sensitive and conscious of our obligation to create a community of nonviolence in thought, word, and action. It is the way that leads to peace and joy. We are committed as a school to this task."

In all conflict, if we spare the rod in word and deed, especially in the fire of disagreement and in its place offer patient and creative responses, we will liberate ourselves and others from inevitable downward spirals of violence that always "spoil the child" and demean and threatens us all.

8

Silence, Sabbath, and the Sacrifice of Time

THE ACTIVITY THAT MOST unites all human beings is the daily push to survive. We pour out our days to bring in what we need or think we must have, especially if we are not motivated by any "ultimate reasons" to exist. Our most basic instincts drive us to continue this existence, pressed on by the desire for visible signs of security. At times, the planet looks like a giant ant hill with billions of humans all engaged in a determined heave to survive. Such all-consuming activity keeps us from the fear of destitution, fear of ourselves, and fear of the questions that might emerge when we are not in the over-drive of our daily routines. We continue this "steeplechase" because it provides forward momentum and that can give us enough sense of purpose to carry on.

Major risks exist in this compulsory march through life, including getting stuck in the monotonous patterns that we can't break out of, which lead to exhaustion or worse—a mind-set of mediocrity as we charge along paying our bills while passing up passion for the truth. This kind of "career" often ends up in the joyous relief of early retirement from lifelong jobs that have sapped us dry. Like the parable of the sower in Matthew's gospel, the cares of this world can derail life's essential tasks and the critical search for meaning in my existence and its Source.

To get into the deeper realms beyond the commonplace routines, we first need to be aware of the grip these routines have on us. This is true for a community like Agape, dedicated to an active life of nonviolence and daily prayer. We hazard running aground if we don't seek a deeper place and ask the fundamental, existential questions: "Where are we going and why are we going there?"

All World Religions speak of a contemplative need for looking within as the primary source of ultimate meaning. Throughout the history of Christianity, monasticism and the tradition of meditation and silence have established disciplines that aid in this journey of inner awareness and discernment. Historically, serious daily spiritual practice has not been available to the average Christian layperson. In the absence of these spiritual tools we cannot truly discern the purpose and direction of life, which is powerfully illuminated by a steady, aware, inner gaze. So, by default, frenzied outward activity too frequently has become the alpha and omega of our daily grind.

The outer noise of our overcommitted lives in permanent overdrive runs in tandem with the steady sales pitch of commercial media—television, radio and now the Internet, with its infinitely vast cyberspace of temptation. All these forces are the pet projects of minds compulsively thinking and being shaped by "want it now" impatience. We remain remarkably addicted as a culture to a mesmerizing and relentless lure of electronic technology.

Post-modern philosophy is another force at work. This consciousness, so prevalent today, holds that there is no ultimate truth, only some good choices and positions that may be worth mastering. Therefore, we need not "go for broke" for some great ideal, religious principle or engage in regular spiritual practice. Instead, we juggle all these good ideas, not expecting any profound outcome, but settling instead for an adrenalin rush of productivity and financial success navigated principally by the technology of the computer age. We simply need to show up every day and give it our all.

We remain focused on getting ahead—always an American value—by staying deliriously busy. "Busy" is what we are, the hallmark word of these times. The busier we are, the more important we appear, and the more subject to the force of "out into the world and up the ladder" we go. Post-moderns possess very few boundaries when it comes to overwork. More always seems better. But, something sinister lurks beneath this push of our ego ambitions.

Thoreau wrote in the mid-19th century: "Most people live lives of quiet desperation."[54] Does he mean that most people live as if nothing really, ultimately matters? Are we "quiet" in our "desperation" because we believe that there is nothing we can truly change? Without hope, the best we can do is to survive well, if possible, and position our lives with a few key economic advantages. To numb down some of the "desperation" might require significant painkilling distractions. The lure of "busy" keeps us in the game while we consume things, people and information to our advantage. We gradually hinder the human capacity to feel and think at deeper levels.

THE MYSTERY OF SILENCE

Once we decide to step out of this routine, and for a moment leave the inexorable movement of mob-thinking, we begin to slow the pace of years of psychological conditioning. In a place of contemplation, a new person begins to emerge and we notice that our awareness sharpens. When we stop to enter silence, we become still. Layers of stress, fear and want begin to fall away and stillness begins to speak. Thomas Merton writes about this moment: "If our life is poured out in useless words, then we will never hear anything in the depths of our hearts, where Christ lives and speaks in silence."[55] Compulsive thinking and talking is background noise that prevents stillness from speaking from our inmost being, where Jesus, the God who is love, resides and speaks to us. In that still point within, we experience both our truest selves and the truth of God.

According to the teaching of Jesus, that authentic truth can only come from one's soul. Jesus informs Pilate: "For this I was born and for this I came into the world, to bear witness to the truth, let those who have ears, let them hear." (John 18:39) Some translations read: "Everyone who belongs to the truth listens to my voice." When we possess "ears" to hear the truth, we begin to hear the truth only if we strive to live belonging to the truth.

Pilate responds to Jesus, "What is truth?" Pilate had to ask that question because he did not know who Christ was in truth and did not "belong to the truth." For Christians, Jesus is the living truth who resides in the inner heart's core. Gaining access to that in-most being requires a rhythm of regular periods of silence, retreating from the world of time and accomplishment to listen to Jesus, who lives and speaks ever more audibly in stillness than in busyness.

Once we belong to truth, we must commit ourselves to a discipline of regular periods of solitude as they deepen our ability to know what is true. Meditation, in its various forms, is one method of the inner journey that can enlighten our way to truth and modify falsehoods which have conditioned our thinking. There is however, a requirement: a regular schedule of daily, weekly and yearly times in solitude and silence of meditation. But, if we choose to stay within the sway of relentless movement and cacophony, we are likely to succumb to other voices and values that we have all been shaped by—vanity, money and money's close friends—fear of scarcity, compulsive work, and the continual trading of time for money. The inner poverty of silence is the very experience we need to save us from our frantic selves and our sped up, acquisitive lifestyle that "conforms to the values of this world." (Rom. 12:1–2).

SABBATH

One of the most profound ways to offset the frenzied pace of modern living and experience the blessings of being alive is to begin to observe a Sabbath. This time-honored practice finds its origins in the creation story of Genesis and was honed by the people of Israel for thousands of years. The ancient Abrahamic Faith of Judaism is a religion that aims at the sanctification of time, and the weekly Sabbath custom became one of the most strictly observed. From the creation story on forward, God's presence in history becomes holiness in time. God creates the heavens and the earth and all that inhabits the earth (Genesis 1:1). God accomplishes this by word and by deed on the first six days. God then ceases to work and blesses the seventh day; God does not single out a blessing for a temple, an object or a person. God simply blessed the seventh day.

Three primary acts of God occur on that first Sabbath—God finishes, God rests, God blesses. This "time" as a representation of all "time" is now hallowed. Three values of Sabbath exist for those who seek its blessings. First, work is finished and complete. Second, we rest in a joyous satisfaction. Third, we experience this time as sacred. Rabbi Abraham Heschel writes in his classic book, *The Sabbath*, that "The Sabbath is a reminder of two worlds, this world and the world to come. Joy is part of this world; holiness and rest is something of the world to come."[56] No ritual object was required for the first Sabbath; the Sabbath moment was enough . . . just to be alive. "The holiness of Sabbath precedes even the holiness of Israel."[57]

The meaning of the Sabbath is to celebrate time rather than space or the things we make that fill our space. This day speaks of eternal time, time-less time, and spirit in the form of time. To regain the Sabbath today is to regain the most central experience we humans have lost—personal experience of the sacredness of being alive. Spirit-led people most often seek spiritual experience by way of a regular practice. In the case of Sabbath, we remember that God sanctified this day. Now, humankind must again and again commit to observance of this day.

"Eternity utters a day,"[58] Heschel teaches us. A time that is beyond space, is beyond division of past, present and future. Time ceases to be an hourglass—or precious time running down. To take absolute rest is the act at the heart of the Sabbath experience. The ancient Rabbis instructed: "Rest on the Sabbath as if all your work was done. Lay aside all clattering commerce," Rabbi Heschel insists. "Labor is a craft but perfect rest is an art." [59]

LIVING SABBATH TODAY

We at Agape have endeavored to practice this art of rest from sundown Saturday until Monday morning, constituting community Sabbath time. It is an ongoing creative discovery to know the specific standards and prohibitions that might comprise an authentic modern Sabbath.

What does it mean to make our personal world become a day of rest that we allow this day to seep into our very movements, sending its aura of peace out over our entire Sunday? The first classic prohibition is—no customary weekday labor. For these 24 hours, we stop everyday common toil and attempt even to abandon the usual, even the so called "necessary practical chores." But an even subtler stricture lies beneath our attempts to stop the act of working. During this uniquely blessed day, we avoid discussions of work, work loads, work needs, word deadlines, and purchases for work, therefore letting go of every pressing demand, including what we would typically see as work related survival and livelihood demands. Another prohibition? No planning future work projects however fascinating, creative or urgent. Simply put, they can wait until Sabbath is done.

We leave behind the pull of money and resource-driven survival. Traditional orthodox Jews established thirty-nine prohibitions for the Sabbath that included refusal to spend money, use modern technology, or drive automobiles on this consecrated day.

Our community practice hasn't gone that far yet, but our Sabbath experiment is very much informed and inspired by radically clear standards. On this day, we seek joyous release from the stress of commerce, deadlines, purchases and computer use, so that the accompanying spirit of peace permeates our homestead, the tone of the community residences, and those who reside in them. Our practice needs constant refinement as we question: "If the essential spirit of the day is rest, how do we know that we are truly resting?"

One of our interns queried: "Can I work on my car on the Sabbath?" My response: "Please don't." I know that this intern thought that it would be relaxing to tinker with his car. Working on a car, however, requires effort with a specific desired practical outcome—to repair the car. As relaxed an activity as it might seem and however enjoyable, car repair is simply more everyday toil. Observing anyone "working" on the community grounds on Sabbath creates an environment that immediately stimulates thoughts of pressing business and unfinished work. Merely watching someone work violates the necessary restful tone of the seventh day. The art of Sabbath is a precious, exacting and mindful work of art of self-observation that is always in progress.

The essential discipline, like most in the spiritual life, is to be aware. In observing Sabbath, we notice that compulsive place within ourselves that just can't leave all work behind. Letting go of work is an emptying process, a surrendered way of being, and a path we walk that exists without time-driven destinations.

I have found that staying out of the garden on a day of rest is preferable. The garden, for a gardener like me, vibrates with imperfections and unfinished tasks. So I'm content to limit myself to a glimpse of the cultivated greenery only from a safe distance unless I need to harvest some vegetables for my dinner. In and out for dinner vegetables without too much scrutiny is best. Taking off our watches on the seventh day and walking without time into the gadget free natural world is a good Sabbath activity. Alfred Tennyson observed: " . . . Time, a maniac, a maniac scattering dust . . . " Time is flying, or time is dragging, or we are "running out of time." All of these phrases express this worried age. The Sabbath is lived in eternity and its peace trains one's soul to ride more "on top of time" than to be driven by it.

SABBATH SOLITUDE

This continual process of inner awareness begins with slowing down the daily anxieties as much as we can. Serious efforts at retrieving our true minds require a place apart, a prayer-filled berth that is both a sanctuary from the world of addictive habits and a propitious place to do the usually avoided inner work. Just our initial act of stepping off the treadmill of activity immediately provides respite and rest we are too often reluctant to take.

Spending the day in Agape's hermitage can be that place apart, one of our best Sabbath choices. A trek up the hill to our hermitage is a journey that radically slows our hyperactive world from spinning. Opening the hermitage door and stepping across the threshold is to enter the world of protected quiet. Inhabiting a place of prayer for a defined amount of silence offers us a chance to free ourselves from the captivity of time and accomplishment, if only for these precious moments. In this silence, we retreat from the noise of the world—the racket of machines, the press of deadlines, the constant intrusion of cell phones, and the constant raging of nations in conflict.

This prayer hut and its surrounding rustic views of the Quabbin Reservoir watershed remove the cues of work, the shrill sound of phones, the click of computers and the tyrannical tick of the clock. Those sitting in the quiet of the woods, who have the courage to carve out this sparse moment, find that attaining stillness is more mindful effort-less, than stress-effort. Often the meditation consists of just gazing out the window, satisfied that all I have now is enough, that the primacy of God is at the center of all life, and that I can afford to busy myself only with gratitude. On the seventh day of creation, God saw creation as good. (Gen 1: 31) In stepping back into rest in the silence, we can literally see that "it is good."

Jesus doesn't choose to teach a strong Sabbath ethic in the gospels. He came from a Jewish world that faithfully practiced this weekly observance. His concern was that Sabbath had become a rigid rule and that an urgent need for compassionate responses to human needs would be compromised by such a pious and legalized practice of Sabbath. Yes, keep the day holy Jesus instructs, but with this caveat: one profanes the Sabbath by making it an excuse to evade one's moral duty of responding immediately to urgent human need, when this need enters the Sabbath. North American Christianity has first to reclaim Sunday as an inviolable day of rest and then realize that "Sabbath is made for humans, not humans for the Sabbath." (Mark 2:27)

To live in a consciousness of Divine Presence, we must commit ourselves to a spiritual discipline and practice. Think of the pride we Americans take in our conquests, economically and militarily, all accomplished through highly disciplined and daily work of our hands. Uncertain and dangerous forces that we are driven to control with this work of conquest and profit, now control us, and we find ourselves beasts of a terrible burden and lose something of our true selves. Can we have the same commitment to a daily, more ascetic discipline, yet with a very different outcome?

In "conquering the world" we eliminate an essential moral priority: the need to conquer the destructive forces within. To begin this inner revolution of soul requires respite, a time to lie fallow within the embrace of introspective silence, a mysticism that "speaks to us," that re-sharpens our ability to "see." This experience, fundamental to our faith, can be found in abundance within moments of meditative silence each day and once a week in the heaven of Sabbath Day.

SECTION III

Peace in the World

9

Constructive Program

I MET LANZA DEL Vasto at a three-day retreat in 1979 in Groton, Massachusetts. When I left the retreat, I sensed he knew something precious—that Christian non-violence is built with bare hands and is accomplished within the confines of a serious spiritual community. Del Vasto spoke of an exacting, almost primitive life—combining hard, simple, hand-hewn work and a daily schedule of prayer.

The Community of the Ark is an ecumenical community inspired by Lanza's days during the 1930's when he learned nonviolence at the feet of Mahatma Gandhi. To listen to "Shanti- das" ("Servant of Peace" a name given to him by Gandhi) and other community members was to hear powerful testimony depicting a physically demanding yet fiercely convicted life of voluntary poverty. With total commitment to God, their radiant faces disclosed a powerful paradox. They lived the "yes of no."

The "Ark people" spoke about what is possible in a pacifist community and the compelling urgency to live in nonviolence, about a daily fidelity to a vegetarian diet and growing organic food, hatha yoga and regular periods of silent meditation. Although they were Christians, their life was a witness to the fruits of Eastern Religion's influence that pulsated throughout their daily schedule. The primary influence of Gandhian nonviolence and the religions of India opened up a wider sense of spiritual practice in a daily spiritual life. Strict attention to diet, rigorous yet contemplative work of the hands, and daily prayer on a schedule were the themes of their life-giving "yes."

In the narrative of The Ark, one consistently hears Gandhi's message shining through—an urgent necessity of fashioning a nonviolent communal life which he termed "Constructive Program." Relentlessly experimental, Gandhi insisted that: "My optimism rests on my belief in the infinite possibilities of individuals to develop nonviolence. The best preparation for an expression of nonviolence lies in the determined pursuit of constructive program."[60]

His was a call to a single-mindedly unified program—constructing nonviolent livelihood and economics, experimenting in vegetarian dietetics and fasting, creating cottage industries that emphasize hand-made goods and non-coercive child-rearing practices, all of which would have a profound effect on each individual member and on their community. This moment-to-moment pacifism is not singularly focused alone on "storming the Bastille" of what is wrong, but fundamentally says "yes" to a style of virtuous living that is experimentally possible and necessary in training people to become nonviolent in a community of peace.

Shantidas offered a vision of nonviolent Christian community that positions a "yes" at the center of daily activity but also with "no" as equally foundational, and urgently necessary to resist the evil of violence. He explains this practice: "The Arc is engaged in spiritual preparation and all-around education for nonviolence rather than in any particular public action. Our interventions have always been signs and testimony rather than undertakings brought to a successful conclusion. The fact is that in order to *do*, we must first *be*."[61] The human challenge is to manifest the necessary fidelity to live this paradox; the daily saying "yes" to the goodness of life is always informed by the undeniable importance of the "no" to what threatens life.

THE TRADITION OF THE PROPHETIC "NO"

Some of the most disturbing people one could ever hope to meet are the Biblical prophets. With their full fury of divine passion, their words and deeds shatter complacency and bravely unearth the lies of the King. They confront the indifferent faithful with ceaseless dire warnings saying in essence that the world will fall in on you if you don't align yourself with the oppressed poor. If your life doesn't pulsate with justice for the poor, or worse, if you should worship money, remember you will die a painful and meaningless death. All that is high will be brought low, idols of political power will be smashed, and in the end, the Lord alone will be held high.

Ezekiel, Jeremiah and Isaiah warn that to forsake the biblical truth of God's law of love and justice, to burn incense to Baal, risks Divine wrath here on earth. Jesus, following in the line of pre-exilic prophets, rebukes a misguided Peter to— "get behind me Satan." (Mk 9:33) He excoriates as hypocrites the Scribes and the Pharisees, models of the well-respected of the religious class. This prophetic "no," this naming of evil, is seminal. This "no" is primary to religious consciousness. This "no" is Biblical.

Even Gandhi, always the hopeful evangelist of the good that is possible to build, agrees that "non-cooperation with evil is as much a moral obligation as is cooperation with good."[62] Like the prophets, Gandhi was suspicious of morally ambiguous "goodness," warning that "goodness is not so much good if it's not joined with knowledge."[63] This knowledge undoubtedly included awareness of the reality of violent forces that we create and participate in each day. Because we are directly engaged in cooperating with evil, we must heed the prophet's challenge: change or perish. They instruct the wayward faithful to "lift your bundle and leave your land, O city living in a state of siege." (Jer. 10:17) Ethnic cleansing and the indiscriminate and devastating bombing of modern war make the prophets' burning words painfully relevant.

When NATO started its cruel and unnecessary bombing of Serbia in 1998, or when more recently, when the U.S. military invaded Iraq and Afghanistan, was this a time to continue our normal routines? Just living in our own worlds, getting the job done and paying the bills? Is it not the moral equivalent of meeting hungry people and greeting them with: "I wish you well, keep yourself warm and eat plenty?" (James 2:16) Or did the bombing ready us for the searing word of Isaiah and a glimpse of the final destruction brought about by our deluded violence: "The land is burned and the people are like the fuel for fire." (Is 9:19) Bombing a foreign country is the time for emergency measures—praying, fasting, non-cooperating with war-making, and uncompromisingly speaking that one necessary, prophetic word amidst that smoldering ruin of war: "No!"

But what happens if our "no" is disembodied from a spiritual center? Where do we head if our "no" is undisciplined because of a compulsive need to know of and respond to all evil? What can happen if this very essential "no" becomes the whole story? Should this occur, a lethal psychology can inhabit our minds. We become weakened when our fixation on evil leaves us enraged at every heinous detail of every war, every execution, every abortion, every suffering inflicted on the economically oppressed and every accompanying ecological devastation to our environment.

Real hope can be drained out of us unwittingly as we find ourselves collecting more statistics on the most recent explosion of darkness, numbed by the relentless media stories that habitually feed us disempowering, hopeless scenarios. Indeed, our worldview can take the lead from our 24/7 news culture that often appears to be in love with tragedy.

Walter Wink has a phrase of warning for any resister who has spent too many "unprotected" hours protesting in front of The Pentagon, or watching newscasts, or reading too many newspaper headlines: "contagion of evil." He observes that "Our very identities are often defined by our resistance to evil, but the struggle against evil can make us evil."[64] "Evil is a contagion. Nobody grapples with it without contagion."[65] The very sight of evil kindles evil in the soul, wrote Jung. "Even a saint would have to pray unceasingly for the souls of Hitler and Himmler, the Gestapo and the SS, in order to repair without delay the damage done to his own soul[66] by viewing the atrocities."[67] Without a spiritual discipline of vigilance, our essential need to have hope in the human experiment is compromised. What often results is an inability to acknowledge the plank in our own eyes that darken our sense of what is true, thus blinding us to the same demons we seek to resist that gradually inhabit our own hearts. To affirm the life vision we need to build, we must include a comprehensive program, a vision of hope in the life we have been given, trusting in the Divine plan while fully cognizant of how the dark facts of our human condition come into play that can be a threat to our sense of hope. "Be joyful, though you have considered all the facts," entreats Wendell Berry.[68]

THE YES: COOPERATING WITH GOOD

A constructive program will discipline our use of time and protect us from the paralysis caused by the seemingly limitless, overwhelming and unintegrated data on the casualties and economic injustice of war and the incumbent human and environmental destruction caused by our first world lifestyle. Gandhi, who continually communed with the poor, observes: "The best preparation for the expression of nonviolence lies in the determined pursuit of the constructive program . . . that person who has no faith in the constructive program has no concrete feeling for the starved millions."[69]

The "yes" of constructing a life's plan needs to concretely address economic injustice in an effort to overturn those injustices done to the poor, powerless masses. The "yes" of a constructive program demonstrates solidarity with the underclass and fundamentally serves the needs of others.

Good social analysis and an oppositional stance to injustice are best utilized by *living* the alternative. If goodness needs knowledge and wisdom, then facts of our U.S. culture's wrongdoing are informative: just 4% of the world's population, we consume over 25% of the world's oil[70] while simultaneously finding ourselves involved in continual resource wars and occupation in the oil-rich Middle East at least since 1991. Approximately $925 billion a year is spent on the military in the U.S.[71] Having inherited empire mores established by Europeans who seemingly weren't concerned that they were plundering the things of earth and oppressing its native people, how do we incorporate this knowledge to inform the way we operate each day? How do these hard facts inform the way we choose to live?

Should we not seek good human work in a simple, wholesome environment? The environment of work blesses us and further blesses the outcome of the work. A constructive program based on "good work" and a "life-enhancing product" is a means towards a perfection of our human character away from destructive and acquisitive forces of possessiveness and compulsive work which inevitably lead to greed and coercive workplace hierarchies. In their place, we employ the virtuous tools of peace and simplicity.

Economist, E.F. Schumacher, writing on the subject of Buddhist economics and the qualities of good work, states that all Buddhist ideas on work and economics rely on simplicity and nonviolence. Buddhist simplicity is based on the conservation of means, maximizing satisfactory results. "Consumption is merely a means to human well-being; the aim is to obtain maximum well-being with minimum consumption" and when producing items, "using the smallest amounts of materials with the fewest inputs of toil.[72] The less toil, the more time and strength are left for artistic creativity. The lower the rate of our consumption, the higher the human satisfaction."[73] "The more modest the use of resources, the less likely to be at each other's throats than people depending upon a high rate of consumption."[74]

CONSTRUCTIVE PROGRAM AND THE INNER REVOLUTION

The Chinese wisdom found in the second chapter of the Tao Te Ching states: "The most important thing to *do* is to *be*." This remains a hard wisdom for the Western mind to hear, so compulsive are we about doing . . .

and overdoing. As Americans, our dominant philosophical and practical contribution to the cultures of the world tends toward the pragmatic. We pride ourselves on what we *do*, on those methods that "work profitably." We want quick access to what works. We are on a frantic search to develop new technology that prizes speed and efficiency by asking only one question of it: Can this technology get the job done faster? Gandhi, on the other hand, warns that "good travels at a snail's pace."

The desire for peaceful work brings us face to face with a terrible dilemma—our hyperactive selves. Even to keep the peace initiatives moving at a good clip, we often prefer not to spend precious time turning the searchlight within, for fear we will discover too many formidable traffic jams inside us. So, in our anxiety, we blast the searchlight out there, only to learn of additional lies uttered by our governments and corporations which reassure us that collecting more details regarding their wrongs will finally liberate us from all of this evil. The evil that we feel we need to resist seems to be "out there." To quicken our steps in "fighting" against evil, we continually force ourselves to swallow more of these hard facts. We deny the rage and fantasies of revenge that burn inside us as daily as we face the blatant spin of distortions by media and the cruel political manipulation all around us.

Without denying the validity of social analysis, Shantidas' community vision seems to stand on the primacy of Gandhi's insistence on constructive program. "When the Tree of Life has been found again, our acts will fall from it like ripe fruit full of savor."[75] Again, the bedrock maxim is that virtuous living comes from love that is radical enough to bring about an authentic way of being and pattern of living that realistically addresses the signs of times.

Shantidas puts the role of protesting violence in perspective as he outlines The Ark's constructive program. "Much more than going into the streets distributing tracts . . . being beaten and jailed (all of which is good and which we gladly do), the most significant testimony in favor of non-violence and truth is living— living a life that is one . . . from prayer and meditation . . . to laboring for our daily bread . . . living a life in which there is no unfairness. What matters is to be sure that such a life is possible. What matters is to discover where there is a nonviolent economy, a nonviolent authority without coercion, nonviolent farming, diet, and medicine. What matters most is to be sure that all violence of deed, even of thought, even hidden and disguised has been weeded out of our religious life."[76]

The greatest field of battle depicted here is not in war-torn Africa, Palestine, Iraq or Afghanistan or even the threat of nuclear holocaust, but the strife within us and our communities. The corollary to this maxim is to have the courage to confront our own delusions. This interior work, done in a soulful spirit, is not the only work we must do. It is simply the only indispensable work of any constructive program.

Robert Thurman, Tibetan Buddhist scholar, who writes about living in this transforming spirit, in his book *Inner Revolution*, asks if it is possible to take "our specific cleverness and ingenuity, and turn our attention toward the inner self the way we have turned it so successfully on outer nature. Can we investigate our lethal passions and their instinctual foundations, and find out precisely how they work and use us as their instruments? Why not engineer spiritual balance and harmony? Then we can devise technologies and arts to conquer these passions and transmute them into useful energies."[77]

THE VISION OF CONSTRUCTIVE PROGRAM

When Jesus was told that his mother and brothers were outside waiting for him, he uttered a curious reply: "My mother and brothers are those that hear the word of God and put it into practice."(Luke 8:21) Aside from the consistent fact that Jesus is tough on conventionally defined "family values," he teaches us that the focus of a true life of faith is placed directly on hearing and doing. Biblically inspired doing can become a fine work of art, or the ground of truth for an alternative life, one founded on our understanding of a loving God.

Gandhi possessed a life-long dream: to develop self-contained villages based primarily on agriculture and cottage industries aided with only simple, inexpensive, usually hand-operated machines. These low-tech machines required muscle and ingenuity and needed no policing or high tech maintenance. Gandhi consistently reminded us of the necessity and inherent dignity of physical labor. "The supreme consideration is the human being. The machine should not atrophy our limbs. What I object to is the 'craze' for machinery. People go on saving labor till thousands are without work and die of starvation.[78] What I insist on is the necessity of physical labor; no person should be free from that obligation. It will improve not only our bodies but the quality of our intellectual output."[79]

What would a constructive program look like today? One model would be an increase in the number of smaller, decentralized villages and intentional communities located in naturally healthy surroundings with people living more deliberately, developing more of a social conscience and responsibility, working for the common good and not just for our rug-ged individual good. In these lifestyle laboratories of experimentation, we can learn nonviolent alternatives in all conflicts and periodically mount the campaigns as needed to keep our own bodies healthy, but also to be concerned about the health of our precious air, earth, water and animal life. A true constructive program for these times will always unite a creative ten-sion between the apparent opposites of the "No to the violence against all life" and the "Yes to all the life that is in and around us." An excerpt from a poem Daniel Berrigan penned to our community celebrates this marriage:

> *So here's to you and modest means*
> *you are so much of little.*
> *The yes of no*
> *and tears unchecked and joys hard won*[80]

10

Sacrifice and Social Change

I ATTENDED MY FIRST major peace rally on Boston Common in October of 1969. I still remember the excitement, the youthful solidarity and the feelings of power from the sheer numbers and heady times as the war in Vietnam began to lose political support and being "anti-war" was becoming a dominant political force. Since the Civil Rights March on Washington in 1963, protest movements have had a tradition of building momentum with the dissenting position-takers packing the streets of the Capitol, New York City or a presence at the United Nations. For the last four decades, when a call went out to stand against plans for wars, to resist wars in progress and the spread of nuclear weapons, many of us have tried to respond.

Two ongoing problems persist, however, when large numbers take to the streets. The first is a suspicion most Americans have of large protest rallies, which appear undisciplined and disunited, or as angry masses of people venting their frustration. Without the necessary spiritual self-restraint and gentleness to effect social change, mass rallies often convey to protesters a false and ephemeral sense of power that can descend into self-serving, self-gratification and speaking only to the choir. To communicate effectively, mass gatherings need to exude the conviction and centeredness of nonviolent peace to both to the police and the general public. An authentic nonviolent witness would eliminate the need for security protection by police. Rather, nonviolent activists are trained to "police" themselves.

A second problem is the temptation for the protest gathering to become a carnival of celebration for the anti-war tribe. Christopher Shirtsleeve, a Brown University student, joined Agape and other peace communities in an act of civil disobedience at Natick Weapons Labs on the day when the U.S. invaded Iraq in 2003. He wanted to join us to do something risky and add his voice to those saying "No to the invasion" in a dramatic and prophetic way. He condemned the peace rallies that publicly opposed the year-long run up to the Iraq invasion as "too much like a party". Indeed, this young activist had a point—to stop this war, something more committed and costly was needed.

Throughout the wars of the last eight years, a consistent anti-war cry of "End the Occupation of Iraq and Afghanistan" and "Bring the Troops Home Now" at the many rallies I attended seemed to be energizing festivals of anti-U.S. foreign policy theatrics and inspired oratory. Historically, rallies aren't a time for introspection, and over the last twenty years, I've observed the demise of media coverage of protests, combined with the reality that the microphone for peace is devalued and has increasingly limited power to influence Washington.

One month prior to the invasion of Iraq in March 2003, protestors worldwide took to the streets to voice their strong opposition. What effect did these protest rallies have before, during and after the invasion? Inspired as they were, they failed to stop or even slow the plans to invade Iraq. Bush proceeded almost as if he had unanimous international backing. After the Iraq invasion, he stayed on this war path in spite of this continued worldwide opposition, and in spite of a military quagmire, Iraq prison scandals and diminishing support for the war itself. He strove on—even in the face of hurricane disasters that clearly indicate that money and attention were squandered fighting the enemies we have created in Iraq. When Hurricane Katrina arrived, Washington was preoccupied. Plenty of money and personnel for war ($1 trillion spent on the Iraq war alone as of 2010) appeared, while urgent human needs nationally went begging, even in such an extreme national catastrophe as Katrina.

TAX DOLLARS AND SACRIFICE

I have spoken to many American combat soldiers who have returned from Iraq complaining bitterly that the only Americans who sacrificed anything for this war are those in combat. Nonetheless, many soldiers seem oblivious to the fact that Bush and now Obama conduct illegal, unwinnable wars without end, multiplying terrorism, requiring no immediate or long-term hardship from the average citizens, other than surrendering their tax dollars, which has a profoundly debilitating effect on the economy.

Americans are not about to line up in government-controlled gas or food rationing lines to sacrifice for these wars. Why? The rationale for the war in Iraq, far-fetched from the beginning, is now an official lie. In recent wars since World War II, Americans have been willing to spend their hard-earned tax money but suffer only *limited* casualties. Who then, ends up sacrificing? Those without power—the poor and working class who are the first to be enticed into the military, while the remaining involuntarily poor are forced to scrounge for work and public funds as local budgets are ravaged by military spending at nearly one trillion a year as of 2011.[81]

But to the vast majority who cry, "Bring the Troops Home Now!" we might pose a question: Are we willing to sacrifice anything to that end, risk any hurt, and do without—to back up our powerful rally numbers and impassioned rhetoric? Is the peace movement itself too ambivalent about sacrifice in a way similar to the body politic which wants only to sacrifice tax dollars and a limited number of soldiers and casualties to this war? Will war end and peace be established by crowding into Washington D.C. on Saturday, our off day, only to show up Monday morning at work, without any commitment to a costly belief and strategy, and without any of us significantly changed?

On February 15, 2003, one month before the invasion of Iraq, our community joined several hundred thousand protestors who packed into midtown Manhattan to voice strong opposition to the imminent decision to launch an attack on Iraq. After hours of inspired speeches given by the likes of Bishop Desmond Tutu, songs by Pete Seeger, and soulful prayers from those representing the Abrahamic religions, we all dutifully filed out of the city, content that we had done something. Imagine if tens of thousands or merely five thousand people, (a very small percentage of the total rally) had chosen to stay in midtown throughout the weekend until commerce started up again Monday morning?

At rally's end, why didn't all 200,000 of us just sit down? Were we content to just have another anti-war party? Do we really believe that our momentary numbers will scare our leaders straight? It has become painfully clear that something more expensive and dear to us needs to be wagered to live without war.

This bloody truth calls us back to the Biblical Prophets. Walter Brueggemann, in *The Prophetic Imagination*, speaks to this sense of urgency. "Passion is the primary prophetic agenda . . . it is the capacity . . . to suffer, to die. To feel is the enemy of imperial reality. Imperial economics is designed to keep people satiated so that they do not notice; its politics blocks out the cries of the denied ones, its religion are an opiate."[82] We in North America experience "ourselves in a religion of immanence and accessibility, in which God is so present to us that God's abrasiveness, God's absence, God's banishment are not noticed, and the problem is reduced to psychology."[83]

The empowered word, fearlessly spoken, yields to the promise of something new. If we spend protest weekends in Washington D.C. or New York City, such protest precludes—sacrifice for something new. Peace rallies, void of a necessary risk, only celebrate an America viewed from the vantage point of war presidents Lyndon Johnson to George W. Bush to Barack Obama, as a demonstration of the greatness of America in offering freedom of assembly and freedom of speech. After the euphoria of the mass protest, solidarity begins to fade, and something primary is lost as early as the trip home. We must ask ourselves: Is this mass movement simply a sign of collective frustration with *this* war or are we ready as people of faith, as people of peace, to withdraw our support for all that makes for *every* war?

RISKING SOMETHING FOR PEACE

When I traveled through Iran in 1972, the Shah of Iran was at the height of his power with close ties to the US. Young Iranians were in almost total despair, feeling powerless to speak or to change the corrupt and repressive dictatorship of the Shah, and despondent at their lack of work and inability to leave their country. Over the next seven years, people began to speak out and to chance life-threatening public demonstrations. Still, politics remained largely unchanged.

In 1979, people refused to go to work in the oil fields. The Shah was out of the country at the time and was never able to return. This work stoppage was the required sacrifice. It is a fact that Gandhi never attended peace rallies because he was too busy convincing India's poor to stop hugging the chains that bound them. During the Salt March, while pausing from the official daily walk, he went from town to town trying to convince those Indians who were working for the British to quit. Even dire financial necessity, he argued, isn't a viable moral reason for giving one's allegiance and labor to the oppressor.

Paul's letter to the Romans instructs: "Do not conform yourselves to the standards of this world but let God transform you inwardly by a complete change of your mind." (Romans 12:1–2) War has always been a standard of this world. Love of power over others is another great lure, the "gold standard of the world." But as God "transforms us," we engage in the miraculous—"a complete change of mind," enabling us to *see* the truth—that every war is cruel. War is a lethal human passion to kill and torture the enemy, to inflict trauma on the enemy's children, and unavoidably kill innocents in the crossfire. Now with modern weapon systems, we also poison enemy land with nuclear contaminants that will last for millions of years.

Jesus, the One with ultimate authority, commands us to love. But certainly, mass homicide isn't love. With all these wars being prepared and waged in our midst, the Christian church is too often silent. The truth is that today, our Christian churches are not a counter-sign to wealth and privilege. Rather, church people are preoccupied with enjoying the spoils of our economic and military empire, not with questioning it. We have become deaf to the prophetic voice of the prophetic God.

As Jesus began his public ministry, Satan looked to derail it by offering Jesus all the wealth of this world if only he would bow down to Satan. Jesus answers: "Be gone Satan, for it is written you shall worship the Lord and the Lord alone shall you serve." (Matt 4:8–11) Jesus' Divine Law of love sheds light on the realization that the cruelty of war is an eternal deathtrap. And yet, isn't war simply the evil front man that masks the real satanic force immersed deep in the hearts of us all? And what of fear, the veil covering the truth of the futility of all war?

POLITICAL CONSENT AND FEAR OF SANCTION

Gene Sharp, in his book *The Politics of Nonviolent Action*, outlines four major reasons for political obedience: habit, fear of sanctions, moral obligation and self-interest.[84] Habit keeps the tradition of good order in this country. In North America, political losers gracefully concede, and the country is united. Lock-step obedience is also a habit that necessitates relinquishing fidelity to truth. Election Day etiquette for those who lose is to rise above political differences and concede defeat.

Losers gracefully concede, even when there is evidence of election fraud, i.e. the 2000 and 2004 presidential elections or the Supreme Court interceding and declaring the winner in 2000. We are indoctrinated to "obey the system". To refuse obedience or to contest the outcome of an election is considered sore losing. That refusal is also a direct threat to those who wield power behind the scenes. Fear of the suffering of sanctions that those in power can inflict is what keeps the opposition quiet. To oppose election results legally or to refuse to obey an elected leader, usually comes with a price. One could be punished politically, jailed, and socially ostracized. Disobedience to the system can bring careers to an end or worse, banishment from the mainstream, with all of its microphones, perks and advantages.

To stay on the team, to have a future, we obey. But, in this society, self-interest is the chief reason for our consent. Political power is achieved when those in power cater to the economic needs and desires of the body politic. As long as the majority is assured of economic security with all its guarantees, there is no burning incentive for dissent or non-cooperation. The vast majority of Americans—left, right, and center—live in dread of losing these advantages that they have worked so hard to put into place. We will complain bitterly how bad things are, but we won't risk our privileged status, steady income, and social standing, even for what we know is true, if it is deemed too costly.

Speaking truth to power is common in this culture, but sacrificing for it is uncommon. Historic revolution and non-cooperation campaigns (i.e. Gandhi in India, Civil Rights in the U.S.) are movements that have always come out of the pain of economic injustice, social oppression and a legally permitted racism. Effective non-cooperation comes out of "last resort" dissatisfaction. This "nothing more to lose" state of mind is the precondition for serious risk.

Historically, mass movements of those willing to suffer for the truth don't often come from the middle and upper middle classes. We haven't suffered enough of what the disenfranchised poor have suffered. Such suffering has always been the price of social change.

In 2004 we saw this truth played out in the Ukraine uprising that became known as the "Orange Revolution." The people said "No!" to election results that they believed to be rigged, with thousands filling the downtown square in Kiev for months. Opposition to political corruption hit a tipping point and compelled the people to act fearlessly. Many protestors vigiled and slept in the square in Kiev, committed civil disobedience, but never resorted to violence. Within months, the election results were declared falsified and then reversed.

First world power leads to massive military budgets that propel us into wars that protect first world economic systems whose foundation is oil. Because burning oil packs the atmosphere with carbon dioxide, which unnaturally warms the planet and threatens to flood the world's coastline, creates life-threatening drought, and intensifies the frequency and force of hurricanes and tornadoes, oil boycotts are now the sacrifice whose time has come. Urgent and immediate measures must be undertaken to phase out all dependency on oil and to begin today to embrace alternative renewable energy—wind, solar, hydro, geothermal, vegetable oil for diesel engines, indeed, for any energy that is local, sustainable, kinder to the earth, and affordable. Petroleum is a warlike energy. First we must fight over it; then when we burn it, we do violence to our earth. Yet this poisonous fossil fuel can't survive one day without our economic, political and military support.

Political and economic powers are not taken from us; we give them away. If we continue to consume more than we need and thus burn massive amounts of oil, we effectively authorize our president to wage war. We take back power from political tyrants by withdrawing cooperation from their unjust policies first morally, then economically. The slogan for today is— "No oil, no blood." The question lingers: Can we defect in place, saying "No" economically to our empire in the name of love of the entire world's people and love for our sacred earth?

11

In the Absence of the Sacred

THAT THE HUMAN FORM is sacred, the New Temple is one of the greatest lessons of the Incarnation. But the creation story in Genesis concludes with the whole truth—that all life is good—the natural, the elemental and the human (Gen. 1:31). This fragile web of life is one sacred tapestry, loved into existence. To be a conscious being in human existence is to be gifted with Divine purpose—to know life utterly as God's sacred plan and to protect its holiness with our life. Knowledge of this sacred plan for Christians comes from staying tuned to the biblical story. Given the fragile state of our world, torn by strife and environmental extremity, we may need to call on the biblical vision more than ever to save us from ourselves.

Much has been written this past century on the origin and causes of our culture's social decay. In listening to the prophetic voices which rail against materialism, environmental destruction, economic injustice and the wars that perpetuate economic injustice, questions arise: Why are we humans so centered on the struggle for dominance and the fight to the death over who owns or controls what? Why are our best energies sapped by our insecurities? Why do we live at such variance with the vision of Genesis? Why can't we just accept life as good and divinely ordained and live in cooperation with this vision?

The problem originates with the fact that the vast majority of Americans live their lives in the absence of the sacred. A sense of awe is not experienced in our day-to-day movements. Divine presence is often lost to us in the commercializing of everything. Even the vast and primitive natural world and its wilderness are too often reduced to the escape into an array of vacation lands. Many of our religious services have become obligatory rites. Modern work and livelihood have become mandatory and meaningless routines. Family life and the family's sense of daily connectedness to sacred ritual, symbol and inspired story is at best episodic. As this direct knowledge of the sacred evaporates around us, evil's roots of anxiety begin to thrive.

With no confidence in ultimate good, we look desperately to fill this void. As it opens within us, we turn to something concrete with which to fill it, seeking a measure of security that we can count on. In the absence of the Absolute, the drama of our existence can be plagued by a passion to possess something. To be at peace with our world, we humans require a foothold, a sense that life is secure, that we will be provided for. But if our lives are devoid of profound searching, our most precious hours become dedicated to grasping for something tangible, most commonly, material security.

Yet, putting financial security as a first priority is accompanied by an unsettling fact—not everyone on this planet can have the same access to wealth. If our primary drive is to survive "well" in the material world that is not within reach of everyone, then we become preoccupied with keeping the flow of money and the things it buys coming toward "us" and away from "them." Competition for economic advantage begins to crowd out an authentic search for the spiritual purpose and values that genuinely transform us.

In our ferocious instinct to survive, Jesus offers us a new vantage point. His religious heritage is grounded in the Torah, a tradition which trusts that God provides bountifully, especially in times of extremity. In Exodus, Moses led people who were desperate for water into the desert. Yet, God provides abundantly when Moses "struck the rock of Horeb." (Ex. 17:1f) Further, the Torah is tested in the fires of economic injustice and the excoriating words of the prophet Isaiah: "The spoil of the poor is in your houses." (Is 3:14) Economics is also a central theme in the synoptic gospels, the great ethical teaching book for Christians. Consider one fact: one of ten verses in the synoptics teaches either a warning about wealth or the wrongs of poverty born of injustice. Jesus is relentlessly teaching us to be aware of our "worldly-bound economics" and trust only in God to provide what is truly needed. "Woe to you that are full; blessed are the poor." (Luke 6:20) He counsels his followers to keep their fix on deep things, such as trust, "and don't be anxious about your life, what your livelihood will make, what you are to eat . . . or wear for clothing." (Matt. 6:25) Identify instead, says Jesus, with those that don't have—"sell all your possessions and give alms." (Luke 12:33)

We must abandon ourselves to love, not to worldly cares: "Whosoever of you does not renounce all that you have cannot be my disciple." (Luke 14) Jesus' teachings on wealth and possessions strongly emphasize their centrality in our thoughts and actions; namely that our attitude about money and what we desire to "have" reveals more about us than any other aspect of our lives.

COMPULSIVE IMPULSE TO BUY

Mark Twain wrote for our time with these words: "Civilization is the limitless multiplication of unnecessary necessities." Our experience of raising a teenage daughter in today's climate gave us more of an immediate glimpse than we ever wanted of the hysteria to buy, buy, buy! In today's marketplace, frugal ways are deemed a useless discipline. "Having" is the message that conditions us through the 3,000 advertising messages we receive each day. The result? A tragic distortion of self-aggrandizing self-worth. Human value is pitifully reduced to the status of what we own.

Americans, even those of modest means, watch television and assume that they can have what they see. A friend of very limited income was complaining to me about his teenage daughter constantly asking for money. "When I was a kid, I never asked my father for an extra dollar," he said. "It just wasn't there." The teenager of today spends the same amount yearly of allowance[85] as 80% of the world's population spends just to survive.[86] Our teens beg for a new i-Phone in a world where one-half of its people have never made a phone call.[87] High technology joined to a frantic pace yields a compulsive extravagance; dangerous excess has become the accepted norm, even a birthright entitlement.

The singular emphasis of Jesus is warning us about the perils of wealth and economic injustice which evolved naturally out of his world—a simple hardscrabble agrarian society. From the humblest of environments came this dominant motif. Life was a low-technology void of modern electronics, earth-centered effort. Its ways were simple, direct, physically demanding, and less toxic and overwhelming than today. Day-to-day existence was lived on small-scale toil and thriftiness. Compare this to the stress-laden, money-driven urban world of today with its din of advertising noise and images barraging us from radio and television, convincing us to live beyond our means.

One shudders to think what Jesus and the prophets would say about accepted modern practices of money investing, money lending at interest, gambling with money and being in debilitating credit card debt for lack of money. When the sky is always the limit, then realizing limitless horizons for wealth is considered admirable, a way of ennobling the competitive spirit in this economic horserace of the market. "You are what you have" is the story told on TV shows and movies, along with the various internet sales pitches. Entitlement to having "everything" is the ethos that many children in America are born into. We passively allow TV, media, movies and advertising to "tell our story" about what it means to be human, what we should want and what has value.[88] The fruits of all this? Luxuries have now become needs; we enjoy the illusion of limitless buying power fueled by insatiable material desires satisfied instantly with the swipe of our credit cards—an addictive and dangerous combination indeed. But that has not always been the case.

BUYING BEYOND OUR MEANS

America as a culture of over-consumption originated in the 1920's as a strategy to stimulate a faltering economy. After the short-lived depression of 1920–22, the business community sought to transform economics with a new approach. Unlike generations in preceding decades that prized frugality, purchasing only what they functionally needed and paying only with hard-earned cash, now you could purchase on the "installment plan". This didn't require buying with cash on hand. Going into debt was shameful prior to the 1920's, whereas in the post-World War I era, most citizens began to acclimate themselves to being in debt as America emerged as a leading economic power worldwide.

Buying beyond one's immediate means then became the norm—a "new" propaganda. Advertising budgets tripled from 1918 to 1929. The business community backed by government support inaugurated the campaign of "buy now, pay later" that ushered in a new level of national prosperity.[89]

More was now better, and the power to buy was to become synonymous with happiness and success. This sales pitch in the mass media was "revolutionary." Frugality was now a worn-out, Old World virtue, almost anti-American, while making, spending and consuming more insured a strong national economy. From 1922–1929, the sales of radios jumped from $60 million to $852 million per year. Car production mushroomed from 4,000 in 1900 to 4,800,000 in 1929. Following the trend of indebtedness, 3 out of 4 radios and 3 out of 5 automobiles were purchased on credit.[90] The volume of sales on the New York Stock Exchange leapt from 236 million shares in 1923 to 1,125 million in 1928. People borrowed money and bought more stock. By 1928, the stock market was carrying the whole economy.[91]

Over-consumption and buy now, pay later, were born. Today, we are deliberately taught to want what we don't need, what hadn't occurred to us to want, and what is unhealthy to want—in order to satisfy these ever-increasing "sophisticated" desires that ultimately only serve to increase markets for American corporate profits. The global economy's legacy of success today? Credit card debt is utterly normal and economic bondage is an acceptable tradeoff for the illusion of limitless buying power—a message that has shaped our inner-most thoughts and formed our world view as Americans from our most impressionable years. Two-thirds of American households purchase with credit cards, with the average cardholder debt at $16,000.[92] Mortgage your future for the power to own anything you want *now* and witness the advertising industry explode into a $170 billion a year enterprise.[93]

The profits from so-called prosperity are carefully ear-marked for certain pockets. The current 358 billionaires own $1.1 trillion, equivalent to the income of the world's poorest 45%.[94] More than 3 billion people exist on incomes of less than $2 per day.[95] The 13,000 richest families in America now have almost as much income as the 20 million poorest, and those 13,000 families have incomes 300 times that of average income families.[96] The frenzy to climb and command the global economic ladder is sure to ensure economic slavery for the majority of the world living in miserable need. These statistics represent present day 2012 realities that fuel the passions of "Occupy Movements" worldwide. Most of the world's money and resources are kept tightly at the top.

It's time to take the phrase: "Live simply that others might simply live" off of car bumpers and bring it into our daily living practices. To live a less acquisitive life is not only spiritually beneficial, as it frees us from the slavery of our possessions, but it also frees the poor from the slavery of inflicted poverty. But there is more to consider. We seek a frugal life so that all life has better survival potential now and into the future. Plant life, animals in the wild and fish in the sea, our precious air, water, and earth are threatened by toxic effects of the massive use of our first world technology. The common corporate practices of drilling for fossil fuel, digging for too many raw materials for the production of too many of our gadgets and dumping our excessive waste into water systems and earthen landfills have absolutely no sustainable future.

The most urgent need of American Christians as we move in the 21st century is to rediscover our true selves buried deeply under centuries of the "stuff" of economic privilege, and to reclaim a non-acquisitive, simple living, other-centered faith in the Nonviolent God of Love. Only there will we experience the "security" in the superabundance and interconnected oneness of all this God given life we have been given.

SIMPLICITY STARTS WITH ME

Living in simple harmony with all of creation begins within each individual. A change of mind happens when we begin to listen to the resonance of inner simplicity. If we risk listening to our deep heart's core, we must dare to act on the voice we hear or the truth contained within us will perish. Paul's letter to the Galatians is instructive: "If we live by the Spirit, let us also walk by the Spirit." (Gal. 5:25)

Recently, a group of ten college students came to Agape to work, pray, and discuss nonviolence with our community. Almost all of them remarked that they were "fed up with this crazy world," its fast pace, the money drivenness, the sour fruits of their stress-laden college culture. All of these students in their early 20's were risking this field trip venture, going with what their instincts were telling them, and testing their consciences by pursuing a budding passion—a simpler life. All during their stay, they seemed to experience simplicity as multi-layered; a slower, more peaceful pace of daily activity, working together at satisfying but hard manual labor, relating to a more uncluttered atmosphere that prizes a "noiseless" silence, and experiencing the countercultural power of the "rural plunge" they had chosen to enter. Meditation each day and deep listening to each other during our prayer times and presentations rounded out their experience of community. Glimpsing their true selves underneath mountains of stress, they could see more clearly the possible lifestyle alternatives to this "crazy world of ours."

These young seekers noticed something about living with a spiritual attitude. They began to live each day more deliberately, without frantic scurrying with cell phones jingling, constant Facebook checking and texting and being otherwise glued to a "screen." Instead, they found themselves working their bodies, nourished by the homegrown food they tended. Their smiling faces suggested a human readiness for the simple, the manual, the earthy and the outdoors, in contrast to stale, often window-less air that comes with the perpetual sitting indoors, often in the absence of growing and pulsing life, while habitually connected to a full array of electronic gadgets and in the constant glare of neon lighting.

Modern life, is mixed with a voracious need for things money can buy, the fork in the road which divorces us from a sense of the sacred. I'm always intrigued by young people who come to Agape, so caught in a world of speed and quick results, yet so many are still awake and dissatisfied enough to be questioning it all. By risking a venture to spend five days in a slower, simpler way, they step into a new truth that they were looking for deep down inside. When our inner voice whispers, "simplify," it compels us to do simpler things. Thomas à Kempis offers us a useful hyperbole here: "It is better to practice it than to know how to define it." Doing simple things means living less inside your head. As a group, highly educated by world standards, these students were attempting to live more spiritual lives in community while focusing more in the present moment—quieting and freeing their racing minds from overstimulation, and learning by doing.

Because life is a "thou" and not an "it," we need not be slaves of the "time is money" mindset that robs us of the peace which can only come from trust in the sacredness of things. These young people were relinquish-ing their frenzied ways for a slower, more mindful rhythm. As we worked together to slow our pace, to live more by wholesome, gritty work of our hands, we took our cues from the rhythms of nature. Stepping out of the rat race of "having to have," we were following the lead of the earth around us, observing that her bountifulness never hurries We praised the perfect moments of the sacredness of it all.

12

How Are We to Govern Ourselves?

A PRESIDENTIAL ELECTION YEAR is always a good opportunity to appraise our governance. Because our attention is literally overwhelmed with political images and rhetoric of the candidates, it is essential to grasp the true meaning of all these images. Further, we model to the world our brand of democracy that puts inordinate faith in this process of seating and unseating a president to such an extent that one could easily say that in the United States, our true religion is politics. Voting since 1776 has always been promoted as a cherished right—fundamental to our freedom loving democracy and always the best hedge against oppressive dictatorships and keeping the peace.

When an individual says, "I believe in the power of the vote" or "I believe in representative democracy in this country," the question must be asked, who is the "I" who believes? Is it "I" an American citizen primarily, who happens to be Christian, or is it the "I" the Christian who happens to be a citizen of this country? If I am a Christian, a Christ follower first and foremost, so Jesus represents the deep core of my identity, then it becomes primary that I examine the true nature of the State, governance, and political power to realize fully what I am supporting. Is the spirit of one's Christian faith in harmony with the values of the State? Or is there serious moral dissonance?

ALLEGIANCE TO THE STATE IN THE BIBLE

Biblically, the State and royal power were always a justice concern for the people of Israel. Even when the King was considered divinely ordained, prophets emerged to rail against their injustices. Yet, every King had his prophet, and because they were the voice of ill omen, they were often expelled. Still, their voices were considered that of God; their fiery words of truth burn for us even today.

With Jesus, the view of monarchy suffered a drastic change. Herod the Great, still in power when Jesus was born, was so threatened by the birth of this child that he ordered the murder of all children two years and under. This hostile attitude of a ruling power over and against the mission of this Messiah, plus Herod's desire to eliminate him as an infant, is Jesus' first brush with political power (Matt. 2:13–18). This story leaves one with a deep impression of their different natures—worldly and Divine.

The mission of Jesus was then, as it remains today, to stand against the injustices of the Herods and to establish a reign of God on Earth. The degree to which we identify our lives with Jesus and his spirit of peace will be the degree to which we will progressively become aware of the passion for crucifixion of the truth among ruling powers as they have evolved since Herod.

The next clash we see between the power of Jesus and powers of this world is in his temptation. The devil tempts Jesus (Luke 4:6–7) on a high mountain with "all this power and glory of these kingdoms . . . if you will prostrate yourself before me, it shall be yours." Jacques Ellul illuminates the passage: "The kingdoms of this world are not just the Herod monarchy . . . according to these texts all power and glory of the 'kingdoms,' all that has to do with . . . political authority belongs to the devil . . . Those who hold political power receive it from him and depend on him."[97]

Jesus singularly and irrevocably rejects the offer without denying that Satan holds the power to grant such an offer. The point Jesus makes is simple and leaves a permanent mark on all those who choose to follow him: "Be gone Satan, you shall worship the Lord and the Lord alone shall you serve" (Matt 4:10). That is, the way of Jesus is contrary to the powers of this world, contrary to the advantages of the gold mine of media publicity, contrary to money, "the mother's milk of politics" and what flows with that milk-the bankrolling of the oppressors, and the controlling violence of the privileged elite who govern. Power politics has a taint of corrupt money and self-serving military and police violence.

In the United States, every person elected President since Franklin Roosevelt has been the candidate who spent the greatest amount of money. Was this money well spent in the service of the common good or was it money ill spent with candidates reduced to saying what had to be said to get themselves elected? And whose money was spent on these campaigns? The money of the wealthy classes? Whose best interests are at stake? Add to this fact that every president elected from as far as back as President Washington used war, the threat of war, or some state-sanctioned violence to advance the economic influence of the country in perpetual and fierce political and military competition with other countries.

If our motives are elevated, like changing injustice through elected officials, then becoming like the Roman Empire is no way of resisting the injustices of the Roman Empire. In governance, like other life choices, we become what we value. Most Americans believe that in electoral politics, even hardball politics, we exercise the major influence for good on the "polis." But what are the means used to achieve these political ends? The forces of the State, whether democratic or dictatorial, impose their plans through controlling, dominating, and defeating the opposition. If the authority of the gospel is our true authority, the forces of good are counter to dominating and "winning." They embody the cross of love, other centered compassions, and prophetic truth. In other words—nonviolent Agape love.

Church of the Brethren teacher and pacifist Vernard Eller writes in *Christian Anarchy*, "For this (political) world of the humanly great is and remains the cause of all misery, those 'well intentioned' people, those 'good' Kings."[98] There is another kind of non-coercive politics with Jesus at the center. "Rather than taking sides, this politics would be, in a non-partisan way, critical of *all* adversary contests and power plays. It would be a politics of servant ministry completely ignoring party lines—a politics intent on mediation and the reconciling of adversaries instead of supporting the triumph of one over the other."[99]

Again, we become what we value. Gandhi, a veteran of forty years of insider politics in India, after choosing to step down from advising the Congress Party, issued an ominous warning: "We must stay altogether aloof from power politics; anyone who goes into it is contaminated."[100] This "contamination" caused by a thirst for power is the antithesis of unarmed love that serves the common good. In our Federal system, this degrading force is expressed in the continual justification of "necessary military and State violence" in a futile effort to control humanity's lethal tendencies to harm and kill. In this mindset, "legal" violence will always redeem "illegal" violence.

FIGHTING VIOLENCE WITH VIOLENCE

Barack Obama, a man of considerable intelligence, a man capable of simple compassion, a person of color who is profoundly aware of the suffering of race prejudice, is at the same time tragically blinded by the power of his own office as he advocates the big three—(1.) War (when necessary for our national security interests) (2.) Abortion (up to the third trimester), and (3.) The Death Penalty (even without due process as in the assassination of Osama Bin Laden). His presidency is in stark contrast to St. Paul's echo of Jesus' counsel: "If your enemy is hungry, feed them . . . do not conquer evil with evil, but conquer evil with good." (Rom. 12:20–21)

The best instincts in any president can be contaminated by the hubris of political ambition, the constant demands for violence made by power-driven factions within all governments and the demands for "protection" from a fear-dominated body politic. The life-threatening forces of violence against the poor, the unborn and the so-called enemy cast a dark shadow over our defenseless world. Yet, in humanity's distracted state, this darkness remains invisible to our spiritual and moral senses and is, therefore, hard to resist. It becomes impossible to imagine a political alternative, so we get caught in a death trap, frantically fighting violence with violence, but always on the side of "good."

With the phrase, "The rulers of the nations lord it over them" (Matt 20:20–25), the gospel addresses domination once again. Which one of the sons of Zebedee, James, or John will sit at the right hand of Jesus? The sad, historical truth is that this same ambition will find itself in all "religion" as "religious causes" and will yield to war in the name of God. But how many wars can be waged in the name of Christ's love and rejection of hierarchical domination? Herein lays the conclusion of Jesus: "The Son of Man came to serve, not to be served, and to give his life as a ransom for many." (Matt 20:28) What political party or candidate mirrors this sentiment? When Jesus warns about "lording over them," he says simply, "You will not be like them," clearly stating that one will always look to "serve others." Love, the highest good, is a way of being, not an abstract idea, and to make it operative requires a structure that is not dominated by self-protective fear. Could this love ever flourish in our present structure of politics?

Yet, Jesus will not consider a conventional political revolution. As a prophet, his words afflict the comfortable, but unlike his prophetic forebears, he doesn't continue to rail against the King. Instead, he turns his discontent toward his followers and mainline Judaism, challenging the faithful to be different from the religious norm, chiding "It is mercy I desire, not sacrifice." (Matt.12:7) It was Jesus' way to scuttle the illusion of a corrupt humanity—not just by admonishment and a call to repent, but also by establishing a following on the margins of society, one that rejects the system of authoritarian domination and embraces a vision of Christic love, compassion, and mercy.

It is interesting to note that the mission of Jesus was not to reform the State but to establish a following that was to evolve into a force of nonviolent subcultures-moral atoms found throughout human societies that would influence the faith of these societies in a more life-saving way than the violence of win/lose politics. But, the strength of their effect would result from their being a counter-cultural sign of God's nonviolent love, values in opposition to the State that oppresses and lives under the protection of its military.

In an election year, Daniel Berrigan SJ spoke to the Agape Community laying out what it truly means to "vote." To vote, taken from *votare*, and evolving from the Latin *voveo*, means to vow something, to be devoted to something dear. If our primary identity is interpenetrated with Jesus Christ, then we will be devoted to peace, and that will require a new vantage point to live and express it. Our "vote" will take another form. And the form will take expression in a living experiment-subculture communities that reject all dominative power, no matter how noble the ends, and replace it with the "rule" of the Gospel of love that we can freely choose to live by.

In carrying out policy, the State relies on a system of domination enforced through punishment by law backed by armed police, legal experts, prisons and ultimately instruments of war and execution. In "ruling" through the spirit of the nonviolent Jesus, there would be no governance with the force of hierarchy and no domination of foes—not even by authority of the political coronation or democratic election. Jesus influences through love of all beings, and his "politics" functions principally to meet the direct needs of the marginalized first, but always stands for the absolute compassion that embraces all people, rich and poor.

EVERY DAY IS ELECTION DAY

Nowhere in the gospels are we encouraged to vote for someone who then hires someone else to help others in distress, whether they are elderly, poor, or children at risk. Nowhere in the gospels are we encouraged to pay someone else to do the works of healing, compassion and mercy, while we continue to live our own self-contained lives in reasonable safety from their troubles. This is illuminated when Jesus confronts the professional class and warns, "Woe to you lawyers also! You lay impossible burdens on others but will not lift a finger to lighten them."(Lk. 11:46) Yet the gospels do encourage and command us to put others before us and to assist the neighbor in need. This being true, *every day is Election Day,* and we elect ourselves daily to seek out the truth and to be personally invested in alleviating the unnecessary suffering caused by the affliction of violence and to offer succor to the involuntarily poor in their desperate need.

Without voting for candidates to represent us, decide for us, and appear to do the "necessary" work of human governance and protection from rivals, many Christians still maintain there is no other way to survive and flourish. "If good people don't vote for good policies," the argument goes, "then we will leave the system to evil people who weaken our security and positive influence in the world." Many people of good will vote, contending that they are siding with the lesser of evils, a battleground where standing against the greater evil is a moral and practical necessity.

But isn't a lesser evil still evil? And, is voting the only way to affect the general welfare of all our sisters and brothers? Given the value system of current political parties, is voting the best method to foster New Testament values, which are the truest and most eternal of all values in this world? Or are there other, better ways to affect social change, protect the poor and powerless, and witness to the peace of Jesus, as a true way of peace in this world?

If I choose not to vote, a serious question then remains: What will I do to fulfill my moral responsibility to influence my culture in a direction that is more truthful and aware of its wrongdoing? How can we become more enlightened with more compassionate governance and increase our ability to sustain all life forms on earth?

Because it is impractical to wait for a political mandate of the majority to begin the process of building a nonviolent society, we must initiate a leaven of self-governance that is not merely a pragmatic political plan, but a "witness" by small groups of faith-inspired individuals resisting the self-defeating injustices of our present political and economic domination system. Jesus compares these two forces, saying: "If my kingdom were of this world, my subjects would be fighting to save me from being handed over to the Jews."(Jn.18:36) This is what Walter Wink refers to as the "domination system," a governing through the "protection" of violence.[101] In the next verse, Jesus offers his alternative, "The reason I came into the world was to bear witness to the truth, and anyone committed to the truth hears my voice."(37) His truth is consistently revealed in laying down the sword in all thought, word and deed. Doesn't this teaching seriously indict all governments as we know them?

In the *Book of Revelation*, we have the image of Babylon, a remarkably workable metaphor for our first world empire status today. The inspiration comes as a revelation to John that "Fallen, fallen is Babylon the great. She has become a dwelling place for demons. The merchants of the world have grown rich from the power of her luxury."(18; 2–3) The angel's voice of revelation continues to instruct John and by implication, all of Christendom. "Come out of her, my people, so that you do not partake in her sins." (18:4) The first movement is clear and urgent: "come out." In the spirit of Divine love, first-world Christians need to withdraw their participation in the State's powers to oppress and crucify, especially the poor and marginalized.

As privileged citizens, we know that luxury weakens us spiritually and needs protection militarily. Familiar with the abuses of Rome, the first Christians after Jesus developed a way to relate to the sins of the State. They responded to the call to "come out" of the clutches of this fallen State in order to become a living sign of a community of nonviolent love without trying to compete with, divide and conquer, or overthrow the State and its imperial ways.

So the question is not: "How should we be governed?" We do need some order of governance, but not the kind of rule that comes from the highest echelons of political power downward. Human beings are communal and living and working together requires a common effort for survival. But to establish just social policies for the people, to create a just economic order of resources, and to develop skill at conflict resolution without armed force in the face of life-threatening disagreement, we do require some system of governance.

Gandhi's cornerstone for enlightened governance is "Swaraj," the democracy of self-rule, based on the inner spiritual strength of the people; governance so perfected that national representative government would yield to the local. This kind of direct participatory democracy is one in which "self-reliance is the order of the day, where there are no leaders and no followers, a democracy that could only come from nonviolence."[102] The key question then is: How can we govern ourselves in the midst of this fallen, violence-prone and protected world? In discerning the answer, we must determine how and where we will stand so the God of nonviolent love can redeem us all.

Christians who follow the singular path of Jesus manifest a way of being in this world, a way of self-governing life, which must be successfully lived, in and through a witness grounded in communities trained in the ways of nonviolence. We must patiently trust that God will redeem our violence but only in God's good time. In the interim, the Divine plan needs our cooperation. In that sense, it is true that we humans always get the governance we deserve, pray for, and make possible.

SECTION IV

Peace and War

13

Pacifism and Intervention

TOWARD THE END OF the Bosnian War in 1995, some from our community joined friends in a candlelight vigil to pray for those women in Bosnia who had been raped. Rape was now an official tactic of war. The vigil included a discussion about how we in America were responding to a possibility of intervention in the raging warfare in the former Yugoslavia, where atrocities were hitting an all-time high. The question of intervention usually gains momentum when there is a crisis and a need to act on behalf of the victims of atrocity. In our prayer circle, listening to first-person accounts of the rape victims, many under sixteen, we all felt the deep anguish of powerlessness. In matters of world events, we Americans don't like to feel powerless, and, in our impotence, we are quick to cry out: "How can we stop this torture—now?"

William Kunstler, noted 1960's lawyer and dedicated peace activist, responded for many: "I'm for intervention. I don't think we can sit by while lunatics kill." Our anguish at the uncontrollable horror in Bosnia was intensified by a media onslaught of grim scenes of thousands of dead in Bosnia, the young shot down in the streets, the elderly burning their furniture to survive the cold. In such a media blitz, the American public is drenched in images of slaughter.

Yet, we are never sure of the reasons why the media picks this horror and not others. We singularly advance the cause of justice in key places— Bosnia, Somalia, Kuwait, Iraq and most recently Libya. People become monsters—Saddam, the Serbs, roving gangs in Somalia, Col. Qadaffi. Reasons for military strategies and police actions seem clear-cut, but only in certain countries at certain times. First world superpowers are rarely driven by purely humanitarian impulses, but rather by economic and military ones. Kuwait was oil; Somalia, its strategic location in the Horn of Africa; Iraq, again, oil and the strategic location of the Gulf.

The situation in Bosnia was not an invasion of one country of another, but rather, a civil war among three ethnic groups in Bosnia, aided by their compatriots in Serbia and Croatia. The crisis of mass genocide on both sides in Bosnia and the reports of rape camps drove most Americans to advocate intervention. We often feel similar outrage over reports of "lawless" violence when the so-called "rules of war" are violated. We too often vent our indignation and outrage at atrocity with a military invasion knowing that we are capable of cutting the Saddams of this world to the quick in a matter of weeks.

History shows that we are selective about intervention. Why do we engage the former Yugoslavia directly and not invade Tibet, Myanmar or more recently, Syria? Over recent decades, the ultimate case for intervention could easily have been made in South Africa at the height of apartheid. Why no military intervention then? Do we more closely relate to the horror of white, middle-class, European Bosnians? Isn't the question of justice really: "Why Bosnia and not South Central Los Angeles?" What must the desperate poor in our country think when they see American soldiers, often from the poor classes, going overseas to intervene in war while billions of dollars are spent, and their human needs are left unmet?

Indeed, many who traditionally hold anti-war convictions feel compelled to support military intervention when the oppression seems "unthinkable." At the time of the Bosnian War, even William Sloane Coffin, renowned Christian minister, preacher and anti-war activist commented: "Reluctantly, I think we should intervene militarily." Pacifism and anti-violence absolutes are now seen as unworkable in *this atrocity*. During the Gulf War the Oxford Union Society recanted its total anti-war stance of 1933, calling pacifism "arrogant." Throughout our recent history, the cry goes out: "We can't sit on our hands. We must bomb, strategically; bomb the Serbs back from their invasion of Kosovo; bomb the Libyans loyal to Qaddafi; bomb the Taliban back into Pakistan and out of existence."

INTERVENTION SALVES THE CONSCIENCE

Most Americans carry within them a powerful image of invincible violence that can instantly ruin the plans of any (non-ally) "oppressor." Our
internal world is nurtured by a lifelong conditioning through news media
and politics. As we watched the killing unfold in Bosnia and more recently in Libya and Syria, our feelings of outrage are assuaged by fantasies
of precision bombing—quick, effective, clean, and now with our drone
attacks—no casualties on our side. We go all out for short-term results
such as targeted assassinations and ignore the long-term, sustainable solutions. Anxiety, rage, and powerlessness haunt our inner worlds as we
keep listening to the relentless stories of atrocities without recourse to
military intervention. Just to imagine the possibility of retaliatory strikes
lifts feelings of powerlessness, if just for a moment.

For most Americans, nurtured in power dynamics and retributive
justice, it was a great relief to know that in 1997, U.S.-led U.N. forces could
drive the Serbs out of Kosovo in two weeks. It only took six weeks to force
Saddam to retreat from Kuwait in 1991. The scenario is predictable—a few
casualties on our side proportionate to theirs, while our sense of righteousness is total. In our zeal, very little time is spent weighing the downside of
our attacks: post-traumatic stress disorder suffered on all sides; innocents
traumatized and dying by the thousands, the earth and her ecosystems further mutilated and perhaps destroyed.

If we bomb any unstable region, hatred inevitably increases and the
stage is set for unthinkable future bloodshed. In the intervention mindset,
now is all-important, fantasies of immediate victory, driven into us since
childhood. All those TV plot lines and video games we have ingested convince us of the swiftness and efficacy of might. Throughout most of our formative years, we've been given no spiritual foundation, no nonviolent skills
to deal adequately with perilous political conflict. In our history courses,
we study the victorious accounts of violence; a history always written by
the winners. The critique which shows that wars fought to resolve conflict
inevitably yield to hate-filled counter-violence, then to "greater" wars and
deeper hatred, is nonexistent. The history curriculum of our educational
system K-12 has completely failed to teach the efficacy of the study and
practice of nonviolent conflict resolution.

Christian churches are all but mute, failing to articulate a genuine gospel alternative. Experiencing some of the angst we all feel about mass killing,
the United States Catholic Bishops called on the U.S. to intervene in Bosnia:

"Indifference is unacceptable." But just *how* should we intervene? As Jesus would do, with the power of love? Pope John Paul II echoed the Bishops' plea: "Intervention is obligatory" in Bosnia. Both the Pope and the Bishops implied that they are content to leave intervention methods to the State. The Bishops wrote: "None of these interventions are free of risks or costs." Their subtext is unwritten and unspoken. Aren't they really saying: "In the reality of modern war, we ask women and children to pay the cost with *their* lives? We Bishops will call for war from our safe haven." Aren't church leaders morally obligated to lead us to the light by calling us all to the risk and sacrifice of the cross of Jesus, not to the dark hopelessness of the gun?

In American interventions in Pakistan, Libya, Afghanistan and Iraq, innocents continue to die. This is not justice. Could it ever be Christian? But "Intervene we must," cry religious leaders and politicians alike. U.S. air strikes will bring order from chaos and quiet the collective hysteria we feel when lunatics kill, or so we delude ourselves into thinking. We will label such "lunatics" enemies (such as Qaddafi and Hussein), and kill the killers in order to stop the killing.

An age-old nonviolent adage contends that if the very powerful have a clear recourse to violence and refuse to use it, the result would produce a profound disarmament. If we were to use restraint and alternative means in the face of the temptation to achieve quick military victory, this message would break a terrible cycle. Instead, the powerful nations of the United Nations, led by the U.S., become a reverse symbol of disarmament, using war as a coping mechanism, and often as a first resort.

A look at history shows that political and religious leaders beholden to the influence of wealth and military advantage never submit themselves to a truthful examination of the dynamics of conflict. Those on the top echelons of hierarchy rarely admit to the ultimate futility of violence to sustain a lasting peace. Therefore, we cannot look to these leaders to initiate peace-making solutions. Historically, such initiatives have always been the role of the nonviolent remnant—people of peace, bearing witness in the prophetic tradition.

SUSTAINABLE SOLUTIONS: UNCOMPROMISING NONVIOLENCE

Nonviolence has a biblical etymology. The King James version of the Bible reads: "Ye resist not evil," (Matt. 5:38) meaning, "Don't take revenge on those who wrong you." Nineteenth century figures such as Christian Universalist Minister Adin Ballou and Leo Tolstoy took this phrase and translated it into "non-resistance to evil." Ballou added the term: "Nonresistance to evil by violence."[103] When resisting race prejudice in South Africa, Gandhi coined the word "nonviolence," meaning, "Absorb the violence. Don't reflect it. Return good for evil."

To practice nonviolence against Serbian rapists, Adolph Hitler, Papa Doc, the Haitian dictator, Colonel Qadaffi or Bashir al Assad in Syria is to take their evil politics most seriously. But we are deluded when we foster belief that the use of force against these men will end the raw carnage and insanity of their policies of genocide, torture and rape. Our use of force is myopic, with no vision of the bigger, long-term picture. In our blindness, we fail to see that our strategic, "surgical" violence against "them" will inevitably ricochet.

Dom Helder Camara, pacifist and former Catholic Archbishop of Recife, who worked with the poor in the barrios of Brazil for his entire whole life, offered this analysis: "In the countries where the poor are oppressed by their governments such as central Nicaragua and Afghanistan, is there any other road to liberation other than violence?" He responds from his experience of being shot at by the military; "I pass no judgment on those poor people of good conscience who believe violence is more effective. But I say, go as far as you can with nonviolence. There is no victory over oppression and the structures of injustice without sacrifices, (but) sacrifices accepted in nonviolence are better preparation for the future and for reconciliation than the sacrifices of violence."[104] Liberation struggles have long made a distinction between violence and counter-violence. The victimizer (i.e. a Latin American Oligarchy) initiates with oppressive force, and the victim (the poor and powerless), in desperation, often responds in kind. When asked about the poor using violence against military juntas throughout Latin America, the father of Liberation Theology, Gustavo Gutierrez, comments: "The poor's use of violence is always counter-violence against the army who initiates it. But counter-violence is still violence."[105]

Jacques Ellul illuminates the Biblical history of revenge: "Does anyone ask who started it? That is a false question. Since the days of Cain, there has been no beginning of violence, only a continuous retaliation."[106] Ellul underscores the reality that the strife in places such as Northern Ireland and the Middle East pits opposing factions who each have a story of injustice, reasons for implacable hatred against each other: "*They* are wrong. *They* are intransigent and guilty of starting the cycle of oppressive violence." Hence, "Who is to blame?" is truly a dead-end question. Every violent gesture perpetuates an evil cycle. The choice is only whether to intensify this cycle of violence or discover a spiritually valid and pragmatic alternative.

In the Judeo-Christian tradition, God is both power (Creator) and goodness (Love). Torture or genocide throws our faith into chaos as we witness evil incarnate, uncontrollably large, the heart of darkness. Evils of such magnitude question our belief in God's power to stave off catastrophe. In times of great trial, it is difficult to follow a suffering God through Jesus who does not work in the world through omnipotence and immediate dispatch of the King. The nonviolent God prefers to work invisibly and often painfully through the created world with human hands to achieve the miracle of healing and reconciliation. God's purpose is that we, as God's creation, struggle to fashion and participate in, a community built on the love command that Jesus calls Christians to live. The Divine is not a magician who instantly vanquishes the ugly ways of evil, wherever and whenever it occurs.

Life will not be lived for us by God. At the same time, we are powerless to disarm and reconcile on our own power alone. So, God acts and interacts with us. God created life for the good. The violence of evil is continually brought low by God's "Yes" to humankind in the message of Christ Jesus. Failing to see this fact leaves us continually, yet reluctantly caught in activities that cooperate with evil and actions that escalate hostilities, such as we have done in the former Yugoslavia, and recently in Libya, Iraq and Afghanistan, and in endless other examples throughout history.

Christ did not come to analyze this momentous darkness, or to take sides in religious hatreds or to critique ethnic cleansing. He came to defeat these forces, with love, compassion and mercy, unto death. Power politic solutions seek to refute Jesus' message—that evil can be subdued only by love. Yet, we have many examples of the healing power of nonviolence, when, after starving evil of retaliatory violence, love heals. What is needed most in war and genocide-ravaged countries is healing. From 1991 to 1999, 170,000 Iraqi children under the age of five died as a result of the 1991 Gulf War, due to the poisoned drinking water and the U.S. embargo of medicine to treat dying children with dysentery.[107] In the end, military intervention, for all its dramatic slaying of the "bad guy" only injured and killed. War itself has no power to heal the wounds of hate-filled conflict and no facility to reconcile enemies.

In the early 1960's, young African-Americans sat at lunch counters insisting on integrating restaurants, braved fire hoses smashing water into them at full force, and riot police poised with firearms ready. By not return- ing hostilities, the nonviolent resisters neutralized a potentially murderous retaliation. Further, the nonviolent presence of the protestors revealed to the world, the stark humanity and suffering of the black struggle in a white, racist-dominated culture. Martin Luther King Jr. said of the nonviolent campaigns: "For through violence you may murder the murderer but you can't murder murder. Through violence you may murder the hater but you can't murder hate. Darkness cannot drive out darkness. Only light can do that. So I still stand by nonviolence."[108] This bold gesture requires enormous inner strength—such a large perspective, that when instituted, we see the oppressors' evil tactics worn down and their fear-filled momentum baffled when darkness is met with light.

The hope of non-retaliation is that, in all beings, there is a conscience and the spirit of the Divine, even in the most fallen. Jesus would choose to see that potential in all humanity, even in the lowest Serbian rapist and Rwandan mass murderer. In the faintest whispers of the still small voice within us, the enemy's humanity can be given life. The way to reach the spiritual depths of any person in conflict, especially the predatory enemy, is self-sacrificing, non-retaliatory love. But be aware that certainty of the efficacy of this radical compassion flows only from the courage to act and a leap of faith.

Capitulating to violence is myopically focused on ends. "Let's push the aggressor back. In two weeks, we can obliterate his madness." To choose to discipline our actions with nonviolent love in the present moment is to remain focused on the only force we can control—the means. The fact is, we never will totally achieve the perfect "ends" of God's peaceable kingdom in this life anyway. Nonetheless, while we exist here in the midst of conflict, we do have the choice to coax murderous violence in a reconciling direc- tion with peaceful means.

CREATIVE INTERVENTION

One way to "intervene" in a bloody conflict outside our borders would be to stay home. Fasting and prayer, scripture reminds us, are the only means of exorcising certain intransigent demons. There is littleness in this way, just as there is bombast and ego in the way American generals and military strategists loudly issuing trumpet calls to invade. Prayer and fasting are hidden ways that acknowledge that the most potent forces for good can largely be unseen.

Victims of violence, the raped and massacred are in our midst, residing in our own neighborhoods, and they make a special claim on us, another reason to consider staying home. We are in a better position to know more of the facts of violent conflicts and are more culturally empowered to deal effectively with them when they occur on our own soil.

Creative intervention in the midst of gunfire is also a compelling choice of witness. How conflict is truly resolved once it has begun is simple to state—the only effective peacemaker in any war zone is an unarmed and nonviolent one. Such a presence has been that of the Christian Peacemaker teams and Voices for Creative Nonviolence in conflict region of Israel/Palestine, Iraq and Afghanistan. These veteran peacemakers refuse to take political sides, one against another, and exclude allegiance to any government, especially their own.

Nonviolent intervention carries serious risks and is at times, more dangerous than soldiering. Nonviolent disciples historically are known for their willingness to die unarmed in the midst of killing. Supernatural courage is always a profound and prophetic witness when faith and action unite under the banner of disarmed love that refuses to take up arms.

An illustration of such meaningful witness in dealing with political factions at a local level was the work and witness of European peacemakers, Jean Goss and Hildegard Goss-Mayr. They successfully taught nonviolent spirituality and tactics to Christian religious groups while resisting the oppression of the Marcos regime in the Philippines during the 1980's. The American Friends Service Committee, along with the Mennonite Central Committee, have for decades worked in reconciliation and peace education concentrating on mediation and conflict resolution in war-torn countries throughout the world.

To evangelize a peace education mission is to build an international community of peacemakers, which is perhaps the best long-term solution available to stop wars from starting. To educate for peace is to heal poisoned minds from the temptation to kill. In that spirit, we can then build communities of nonviolence, replacing communities of hate and division. Such community-building is the best chance we have of preventing future Bosnias, Rwandas and Northern Irelands; indeed all ethnic wars and holocausts from happening "over there" or within our own borders.

14

Non-Cooperation with War

MUCH HAS BEEN WRITTEN this past century on the origins and causes of our culture's social decline. In listening to the now familiar railing of the "Occupy Movements" in the U.S. against economic injustice, the disparity of income of rich over poor and the wars that perpetuate economic privilege, the question arises: Why are the best energies of human beings sapped by our insecurities? When the state says, "It's time for war," why are people so quick to nod in agreement?

And what are these threats of war but a stress crack in our nation's security? This fault line permits our military to consider committing the most unspeakable horrors ordered by presidents who appear to the general public as "presidentially reasonable." The body politic nervously watches the general state of alarm, but a majority remains aloof enough from the reality of war, creating a comfortable emotional buffer. It is remarkable how most countries just slide into war. Without officially declaring war, treaties are ripped up, borders are brutally crossed and women and children are sacrificed by the tens of thousands.

Don't such human sacrifices completely break with the vision of Genesis that all life is sacred and that all creation is good? (Gen. 1:31) With all the talk of war, the human form, a sacred "thou," is brutalized, reduced to an "it," a malignant "thing" that can kill or be killed.

This insecure image of life darkens our trust. Must we see life then as full of predators, dangerous episodes, made so by murderous people who require constant vigilance and billions of dollars to control? In a conversation on these themes, Brent, a Vietnam War combat veteran said to me once: "Nothing in my life ever motivated me like knowing someone out there wanted to kill me."

Fear is easily institutionalized. Professor Lynch, my college history professor, commented during a lecture on the rise of Adolph Hitler, "History has proven that if someone can get on a soap box and claim another as bad and threatening, they will always get a following." Fear is easily politicized as well. Tolstoy, in observing the "inner" dynamic of patriotism offers that "governments hatch war independent of the interests of the people."[109]

Those who benefit most from the policies of the state know that the self-interest of maintaining power at the top does not advance the common good of the average citizen. Therefore, the biggest threat to a modern state is its people's awareness of power motives which seek to dominate them. To effectively maintain control, a state has to keep people distracted by creating an enemy threat from outside their borders.

Indeed, Hitler, who knew the value of a steady drip of propaganda, stated: "Lies unremittingly told would one day be believed." Habitually obedient to authority and prone to having suspicion of the foreigner, people surrender taxes and obedience to the state in return for its protection from harm by the "foreigner." Tolstoy, even as a former soldier, saw this patriotism as slavery. The reality is that "War is always pernicious to the people, even when successful."[110] This need for security from harm slips into "love of servitude," an acquiescence to authority in a bomb-proof bunker, built and paid for by the body politic.

Martin Luther King Jr. proclaimed, "Cowardice asks the question—Is it safe?"[111] For King, asking, "Am I safe?" always leads one down the wrong road. The point is that we will never be safe enough from life's uncertainties. Precarious and uncertain, our lives are rife with dangerous unknowns. Will I die tomorrow? Will I receive painful news in the next moment that will change my life drastically, involuntarily and uncontrollably? Although "Am I safe?" is patently the wrong question, it is repeatedly asked, as it speaks to an unstable inner world which belongs to most of us, especially in adversarial conflict.

Our American culture is a perfect teaching of unexamined obsessions regarding safety that leads to a compulsive and warlike need to protect who we are and what we have. Our current strategies include:

1. *Control the enemy.* That person who is a threat, I must control. This is accomplished by forcing a threatening person at gunpoint into a dungeon or killing them if threatening enough. The corollary to this—the more police, the better. Just to see the gun at the hip is enough to reassure many. Take a look at airport security.

2. *Baring our fangs.* Writer Jonathan Schell calls this "the balance of powerlessness."[112] Nuclear weapons are so without adequate definitional horror, that just to have them keeps us too terrorized to use them. Instead of the more disarmed world of Woodrow Wilson, a vision that he elicited from the League of Nations coming out of World War I, we have now created a "safe world" by amassing nuclear holocaust arsenals which wipe out federal budgets and their necessities for the working class and poor. Presidents, prime ministers and kings consider it a price to pay as the mere demonstration of these weapons, so the reasoning goes, deters the enemy from ever attacking.

3. *Living beyond the world's means.* The most reassuring safety feature of our culture is the way we live. Our technological and material dominance of the world is legendary. The Union of Concerned Scientists reported that with less than 5% of the world's population, Americans consume 40% of the world's gasoline, 33% of its paper, 27% of its aluminum, and 19% of its copper. We consume over 120 pounds of raw materials per person, per day, excluding water. We consume 53 times more goods and services than someone from China, 30 times more than someone who lives in India. To give every human on earth an American lifestyle would require four planets. The U.N.'s Environment Program, Global Environment Outlook 2000, states: "A ten-fold reduction in resource consumption in the industrialized countries is a long term target if adequate resources are to be released for the needs of developing countries."[113]

The power to possess constructs an illusory fortress, giving an impression of protection from uncertainty. But this pernicious habit of living beyond the world's means leaves us not only insecure, but fractured and fragmented—hungry for more and trapped by our addictive need to buy more of what is unnecessary.

When John D. Rockefeller was asked how much more wealth he needed to be satisfied, he said, "Just a little bit more." The Truth? Too much is never enough.

ECONOMIC WARFARE

Unjust economic systems need a military to keep financial advantage on the "have" side. Michael Ignatieff of the Kennedy School of Government at Harvard, now a member of the Canadian Parliament, wrote something telling in the *New York Times*: "What word but empire describes the awesome thing America is becoming. It is the only nation that polices the world through five global military commands; maintains more than a million men and women at arms on four continents; deploys carrier battle groups on watch in every ocean; guarantees the survival of countries from Israel to South Korea, drives the wheels of global trade and commerce and fills the hearts and minds of an entire planet with its dreams and desires."[114]

Ignatieff gives us a glimpse of the emperor's sword. "Imperial power means laying down the rules America wants, while exempting itself from other rules" (i.e. Kyoto Protocol on greenhouse gases, International Criminal Court etc.).[115] These "rules" have no teeth unless and until America bares its fangs; total military dominance assures total economic control.

We are not a lowly "empire by conquest," as were our English forebears. Ours is a slow, methodical economic takeover that has been in progress since the end of World War I, dramatically increased after World War II and uncontested since the demise of the Soviet Union. Sole superpower status has been modified by the recent economic ascendancy of China as a world power. This long range, 80-year economic "plan" finds the U.S. today still the top economic/military superpower.

The moral righteousness of this "economic conquest" relies fundamentally on a self-understanding that begins with the first shots fired in "our" Revolution. We are a nation that conceives of itself, almost romantically, as established in just revolt against an empire. We are the ally of freedom everywhere and we think of our nation, in the words of Herman Melville, as "the ark of the liberties of the world."

Our self-image is that of good, freedom-loving people. If some country has to police the world and rule the global economy, we morally qualify ourselves. Who can argue with the imperial ways that exult in free markets, free speech, human rights and democracy? Benevolence toward the foreigner in need, however, is not at the heart of any empire, but instead the self-serving economic interest backed by stark protective violence.

INNER REVOLUTION

The poet, W.H. Auden conveys a riveting truth that relates to our current situation: "We'd rather be ruined than changed. We'd rather die in our dread than climb the cross of the present and let our illusions die."[116] Steadfast in our self-understanding as good people, the mass of Americans remain curiously willing to risk destabilizing the Middle East by the invasions of Iraq and Afghanistan on one end of the military spectrum, and to threaten all life on earth by continuing to make and deploy nuclear weapons on the other end. If we dare "to be changed before ruined," it must begin with the courage to admit one bold fact: If we at some ideal point in our history saw ourselves as a country that was "good at saving the world from murderous dictators" or "protecting the world for freedom and democracy," we must concede that we are not perceived in those terms by most of the nations of the world.

Good only comes from God. This "good" seeks to reassure the other—the "stranger in urgent need," with whom we share this planet. Good doesn't seek to dominate the world with economic hegemony and control. Good doesn't kill innocent civilians by the thousands, even reluctantly, in aggressive wars. Good doesn't cajole the world community into joining in a preemptive war on Iraq, a war whose plan is to send a foreign country into "shock" as the bombing of Hiroshima did the Japanese. Good isn't willing to spend trillions of dollars over ten years to kill people in Iraq and Afghanistan, bringing Saddam and Osama bin Laden to their knees while our inner cities go bankrupt and the people at the bottom starve for want of adequate food, housing, health care, and education.

The terrible suffering created by America's wars is among the most inhumane acts that exist today. We must listen to the warnings of Western European countries, our traditional allies. In a historic public and political opposition to our invasion of Iraq in 2003, many so-called former allies, saw us then as a quick-to-war threat to the stability of the world.

"FEAR NOT"

The 1990's wars in Iraq and Serbia were perceived in this country as invincibly quick and inexpensive, with very little economic hardship stateside and with few casualties to our military. Recent administrations have had a zeal for war that appears almost religious. They proclaim, in essence, that "we," with very little risk to ourselves, will rid the world of "them." After WW I, a question could be asked: When will war ever drive out war? The long arc of U.S. history reveals that because we as a people continue to believe in war and invest in war, war is alive and well and has a firm hold on our politics.

The gospel takes a completely different view: "Those who live by the sword die by the sword." (Matt.26:52) But, we must go deeper than the act of killing. If we seek to end war and killing, we must treat its causes. Therefore, Jesus teaches "Thou shalt not become fearful or angry at another." (Matt. 5:22) So ravaged by self-righteous anger and fear are those leading this country (and those following), that they tragically overlook one spiritual fact: that the evil we hate resides within ourselves. The tendency to commit violence is especially strong in those who lack the courage of introspection to see this. Perhaps we don't venture a look within as a people because we sense intuitively what we will find there—a dreaded fear of the revenge by those we have done violence to and a fixated fear of being killed. George W. Bush continually drummed into the American public: "If we don't stop the terrorists over there, they will follow us home." But even before death lies the most palpable fear, a paralyzing anxiety about someone taking our money and our land.

To this, Jesus offers a radical teaching that opens the door to the truth about us in relation to "the other." "Do not be afraid of those who deprive the body of life, fear those who can destroy both body and soul in hell." (Matt. 11:28) Because we have so few models of voluntary sacrifice and martyrdom, we don't trust that Jesus' words are enough when this, our only body, is threatened. Instead, church and state, in times of "national security crises" seek to deny absolutely any serious wrong-doing in which we are quagmired, hardening our sense of righteousness in the conflict, and convincing us we are trapped in a rigid choice of kill or be killed.

Convinced of war's necessity, avenging the wrongs suffered at the hands of the enemy now becomes a duty, and money is no object. In the wake of September 11, we declared war on terrorism around the world and, like a drunken sea captain, went into the breach. Now, we are no longer a ship of victims, but of heroes. Yet something gnaws at us. We know deep in our hearts that we are preposterously rich and recklessly powerful in a world inhabited by the frustrated and desperately poor and powerless. Our aggression will only succeed in making the world more unsafe by putting the U.S. and its "terrorist" counterparts on a permanent, retaliatory, war-footing.

Ignoring the teaching, "Fear not the threat to the body," leads to treachery of the soul. To practice the truth of this teaching starts not with protecting our safety, but instead with asking: "Of what am I afraid?"

If we ask this question with God at our side, we will begin to liberate ourselves from fear. Dying isn't the problem in the New Testament; the problem is fear of annihilation which leads humans to kill. We practice "fear not," difficult though may be because we believe or seek to believe that "Christ is risen," that there is more than this life. We are spiritually challenged by the reality that there is life beyond the grave and that there is an essential gospel teaching contained in our fear of suffering, and it is not just humiliation. Can we risk ourselves in spite of our fear?

Martin Luther King Jr. advises us how discern the truth within: "Conscience asks the question: Is it right?"[117] This "voice within," informed by the Wisdom of the Divine, becomes "right" or true, not just for me, but for everyone. As a Christian, my formation of conscience is guided by the mind of Christ and is always reaching for what is universally true. We act not because it is safe, but because it is true for all, not just for me.

The New Testament vision of truth concerning war and peace is, fundamentally, that the violence of war is not of God. Only unarmed love can bring true peace, a "peace that the world can't give." (Jn. 14:27). For most of human history, we have been living in a dark ignorance concerning our ability to live in harmony with "the other." The world's peace, a hard fought outer revolution, yields the dead silence of the vanquished enemy. The peace of Christ, a hard fought inner revolution, yields the serene silence of the vanquished "enmity."

Albert Camus called the 20th Century, "the century of fear." Imagine now this astronomical spiral of fear and violence, finding its pinnacle in nuclear standoff—the idea of paralyzing the world's nations with the dread of nuclear annihilation as a way to "keep the peace?" Jonathan Schell analyzes such "peace-keeping war systems" in his essay *No More Unto the Breach: Why War is Futile,* which includes the notion of nuclear weapons as a form of deterrence, to the first world's waging of the people's war. The "people's war" is fought by the oppressed poor in a mismatch against the powerful, finding its origins in Mao's revolutionary peasant villages and Mao's tactics which echo tragically today in the strife of the Middle East with the constant threat of suicide bombing.[118] While the nuclear weapon has provided a potentially catastrophic armed stalemate, now terrorism, in its bloody voice, speaks to the anguish of the powerless poor throughout Arab countries. Whether through high-tech weapons or blunt swords, political history is controlled by violence. A turning point comes Jonathan Schell tells us: "The people's war had a further develop-ment, Gandhi's nonviolent peasant revolution in India."[119]

NON-COOPERATION WITH WAR

For Gandhi, political power did not ultimately reside in a ruling elite backed by big money and weapons or in the revolutionary vanguard few who enlist the poor to fight with counter-violence. The power to control a country's destiny is made or broken by consent of the people every day.

All governments rely on the broad-based cooperation of the governed. Withdraw that, and all of the government's threats of violent sanctions are helpless. Decline the ruler's corrupt power and that government will fall and need not fall in violent overthrow as we witnessed in the demise of the former Soviet Union, the British dominion over India or most recently in Egypt in the overthrow of Hosni Mubarak. When the political will of an unjust government is fixed in the violent direction of a police state, it seems unstoppable. But that is an illusion.

Often, those who stand against corrupt policies of the state feel like vic-tims, powerless to stop the madness of military attack on another country. Gandhi empowers those of conscience by saying that "The business of every God-fearing person is to disassociate oneself from evil with total disregard to consequence."[120] But the historical tragedy shows clearly the opposite—fear of punishing reprisal renders silent the moral voice of the people.

Like the Divine Plan itself, Gandhi's words of courage inspire change and conversion, not ruin, strength to resist a war-like state, not acquies-cence with silence or consent. Haven't we in the U.S. surrendered our coop-eration of the governed, enabling our "imperial business as usual" to gain continuous momentum?

Can we stand against our nation's war-like ways by pulling, at its source, the economic plug; our own passion to "possess" that makes war inevitable? Can we renounce within ourselves the need for economic ad-vantage which makes for perpetual war? The prophetic voice of resistance will cry out from such voluntary divestment.

15

Forgiveness and the Divine Feminine

WHEN I HEAR PEOPLE who have experienced a terrible betrayal say "I have no problem with forgiveness," I sense a deep problem with forgiveness. Of all the virtues in Christianity, mercy comes at the greatest price. It has been wisely stated that if Jesus could be reduced to a word, it would be "mercy." But what Jesus asks is always expensive, and when we are in emotional extremity, many of us know the precious need for mercy, but to practice it is a more elusive thing.

"The quality of mercy is not strained," writes the great Shakespeare. I had an opportunity to enter this most costly truth as I traveled to Dallas to be present at the National Catholic Bishops' Conference in 2002. Our community had been in dialogue with our peace bishop, Thomas Gumbleton about how to be present to the Catholic Church and her bishops in this time of both sexual abuse and the invasion of Afghanistan. After talking with Bishop Gumbleton, we decided to redouble our efforts to bring the message of peace, represented by our community's anti-war position statement: "The Catholic Call to Peacemaking: Living Nonviolence after 9/11" to the Bishops' Conference. Being the only representative from the Agape Community, I knew that advancing our nonviolent position on the current war in Afghanistan would not be easy as the bishops were in great turmoil over recent allegations of sexual abuse in the church hierarchy.

My mission in Texas was to hold the creative tension between these dual crises—the earth-shattering revelations of the sexual abuse of children by hundreds of priests covered up by decades of secrecy and the ongoing spiritual and doctrinal crisis within the church herself, and recent support of the invasion of Afghanistan (and within a short year, Iraq). This long-standing moral crisis created by the Catholic Church's historical support of war was again brought to bear by support of the wholesale killing and injury of Afghan citizens in the "War on Terrorism."

In November 2001, the bishops' overwhelmingly supported the bombing of Afghanistan, and then almost simultaneously found them-selves in the present sex abuse scandal. As we observed the peace issue losing the attention of the faithful peace communities around Agape, we began to wonder, "What are the connections between the abuse of chil-dren and the devastation of this war?"

Many people decided to stay away from the Dallas meeting because of the expected "circus" of loose-cannon protests, name-calling and angry banner-waving. When I arrived on the first day of the conference, I found about thirty people with banners across from the Fairmont Hotel where the bishops were gathered. As predicted, the atmosphere was circus-like. Many homemade signs and much anti-clerical hostility and sarcasm flowed from wounded and abused people who came from all over the country to vent their rage at abusive priests, a rage especially aimed at the bishops accused of cover-ups.

In the midst of this unsettling atmosphere, a 40-year-old father of three, Toby Gilman walked up to me, drawn, he said, to my banner which read: "U.S. Catholics to Our Church—Say No to the War on Terrorism." He spent an hour telling me his own story of sexual abuse by a priest in his family par-ish and the suffering he experienced as a result of going public with his story.

As he spoke, I found myself taken by Toby's centered presence and mature insights concerning his abuse, and his apparent ability to channel his hurt and rage in a reconciling direction. He appeared to be a most spiri-tually healed man, at peace with himself. Toward the end of our conversa-tion he said, "I don't know if I should let the priest who abused me off the hook by forgiving him." The abusive priest was in retirement and hadn't seen Toby since he was a teenager 25 years earlier. He seemed to be asking questions of himself by saying, "Does this priest have to pay for this? Does he owe a debt to society that precludes my forgiving him?" These are ques-tions which speak to the heart of the struggle we all have about justice or bringing people to justice.

FORGIVENESS—TWICE BLESSED

Is forgiveness only a word we admire, or is it a moral necessity, a bold act of surrendered courage with the potential to heal relationships that have been ripped apart by unimaginable abuse? Toby seemed very aware of the risk of letting go of revenge. Could any of us look our abuser in the eye and truly forgive, without expecting anything in return? Further, does the act of mercy let an abusive priest off the hook? Historically and metaphorically, the "hook" is a place in the town square for public humiliation, designed "to teach people a lesson" about their terrible wrongdoing, a practice that tragically betrays the unconditional mercy of Christ.

Can we trust that the disarmed spirit of forgiveness will make all things right without going to the law, which exacts punishment in an effort to neutralize the power of abusers but continues the violence by threatening and inflicting a humiliating suffering on them? Will violence as just punishment ever drive out the gruesome sin of abusive violence? Can vengeful justice truly unleash the healing power of the Divine on the devastating wounds of abuse?

As I talked with Toby, I thought of the inspired words of Martin Luther King, Jr. on the healing role of the victim: "The forgiving act must always be initiated by the person who has been wronged, the victim of some great hurt, the recipient of some torturous injustice, the absorber of some terrible act of oppression. The wrongdoers may request forgiveness. They may even, like the prodigal son, move up some dusty road, their hearts palpitating with the desire for forgiveness. But only the injured neighbor, the loving parent back home, can really pour the warm waters of forgiveness."[121]

So it is the mercy of the victim who frees the victimizer from the prison of the abusive act. The implications of this teaching apply as directly to wars on terrorism as they do child sexual abuse. Toby wasn't sure he was ready to trust such unconditional love, but he was walking with a powerful integrity in that direction.

As the days progressed, the climate at the Bishops' Conference continued to be tense and angry. The anger of a victim can be a notoriously secondary emotion masking the primary emotion, a deep hurt and trauma buried underneath. As Catholics and victims gathered in Dallas from all over the country, I was trying to hear the primary emotion people were truly feeling as we were all faced with such horrible facts. What is the real message behind the chorus that came from the line of protesters, "Arrest the Bishops first", when someone in priestly garb walked in front of the hotel?

As I convened with the people who came from miles away to express their outrage, listening to the various speakers at the Call to Action Conference and meeting with Pax Christi friends from Dallas, I heard one phrase consistently: "Children are not being protected."

A Call to Action woman stated forcefully: "Even before nurturance, the mother's role is to protect." Children had become dangerously vulnerable and then victimized within the trusted confines of the parish. The ground swell of outrage expresses a deep panic and guilt, the most intense emotions a responsible parent can feel. A terrible family "secret" was out in the open.

This abuse and secrecy could not have been maintained if not for one basic fact—our church has too many "fathers" and not an equal number of "mothers." This all-male gender imbalance with its secrecy, authoritarianism and the almost tribal image-protecting is in desperate need of the feminine impulse, a maternal instinct to keep it from its horrific secrecy, protecting sexual pathology. Women who attended the conference in Texas saw the problem as primarily a matter of this gender imbalance saying, "Both the abuse and the cover-up wouldn't have happened if women were equal partners in the church at all levels."

So let's take the question of children's need for safety seriously. For most adults, it is almost in our DNA to get between an abuser and child to protect them, even at risk to self. But now a deeper question emerges: Are we passionate about protecting our nation's children only, or are we equally passionate about protecting children in every country, culture, and ethnic background? And from what violence are we protecting them? When we seek to protect the vulnerable, what places children most at risk?

WAR IS CHILD ABUSE

Whether inside or outside one's home, war is the most lethal form of child abuse. Attending to the sexual abuse by priests focuses on the immediate danger to our children—urgently and understandably. Ultimate protection is axiomatic. But as we gradually back away from powerful emotions in response to sexual pathology and the obvious present need to protect *our own* children from it, we might ask ourselves: Shouldn't children *everywhere* be protected from all harmful violence?

Millions of Americans, Iraqis and Afghans have been killed, wounded, and traumatized since 2001. How many were children and their protectors—their mothers? In modern war, the safest place can be in the military, while the homes and neighborhoods where civilians and children reside are a predictably deadly place. Over 20,000 innocents have been killed in Afghanistan.[122] How many were children? As the 12th year of the war in Afghanistan rages on, The Emergency Hospital, the largest hospital in the Kabul area that takes the wounded from both sides recently reported that over 40% of the war victims are children. Of the 1,864 patients admitted, more than half were children under fourteen.[123] In May 2012, Syrian forces fired on civilians, killing 92, including 32 children.[124] An estimated 1,620 children have been killed in Palestine since 1987.[125] When the casualties are counted, war is not just abuse, but a death sentence and torture chamber for children.

Add to the death sentence, the long-term effects of this abuse on those wounded who must go on living. How many children have been injured, crippled and traumatized by warring factions? How many children have been convinced to hate the enemy because of the horrifying effects of their bombs and guns? How many children grow up with a dreadful fear of life because their world is so poisoned by the adult language of hate and rationales for "just" wars? How many of these miracles we call children end up marching right into the ranks of the so-called "terrorists" because they weren't shielded from war's horrors?

This tragic reality has plagued human cultures throughout the long, painful history of bloodletting. To protect all children requires an unwavering rejection of war-like behavior that sacrifices the young to the ranks of rigid religion and violence-filled "theology." We must stop "arming" the world with children who are, in reality, suffering post-traumatic stress disorder.

This insight doesn't minimize the terrible injustice and violence of sexual abuse of minors within the church and the urgent need to respond to it with the most immediate protective measures. It is simply to say that when it comes to children at risk, war has no equal in placing children at the most lethal risk imaginable, psychologically and physically. Children on either side of the conflict who lose their fathers or mothers to combat or see them return from combat, suffering the severe psychological damage of post-traumatic stress disorder, will also experience trauma.

For the past five years, we at Agape have been helping an Iraqi family that suffered tragically from a mistaken U.S. military attack at a checkpoint in Mosul, Iraq. The mother of two boys was killed instantly. The father, shot by our military and permanently injured, succeeded in saving the life of his son Omar who was burned over 60% of his body. The other son, Ali, was unharmed physically. All three are living in the U.S. where Omar and his father, Sabah, are receiving medical treatment.

Aside from Sabah's serious life-threatening bacterial infections from shrapnel, the major wound they all suffer is the trauma from their attack and their displacement in a foreign country. We can see in the boys' faces, the hurt and frustration in their eyes, the tragic effect of being robbed of their mother's care. The "child abuse of war" continues to make their anger and frustration ongoing and often uncontrollable.

Unlike sexual abuse, which now the Church has been forced to condemn publicly, Catholic hierarchs are still debating the efficacy of the Just War Theory, still risking children's lives on the front lines because they cling to rationalizations about the necessity and efficacy of war. All war engaged in by the United States since World War II has been considered "theologically just" by most of our church leaders who regret, we assume the inevitable collateral damage to innocents. The Just War Theory does acknowledge the possibility of collateral damage in a "just war."

The war remains "just" if all other criteria are met because the killing of innocents was not intended. The heartless audacity of this doctrine which accepts the inevitability of the killing of noncombatants in any "necessary" war stands out in its moral dissonance within the vast body of morals and ethics of World's Religions. How horrified God must be at humans justifying, if even regretfully, the killing of innocents and children. And this is precisely what the Catholic Church blesses or allows when it gives its allegiance to *any* modern war.

The truth is that the Just War Theory is so small-minded and morally bankrupt that it belongs alongside the Flat Earth Theory. No biblical justice can ever exist in the "justified killing" or infliction of trauma on children. Clearly, sacrificing the lives and well-being of the world's children fails to hold them up as innocent wonders of God, whom Jesus in turn holds up for us adults to emulate: "Humble yourselves like a child, for they are the greatest in the kingdom of Heaven." (Matt 18:4)

As the tragic history of war extends into the 21st Century, children's chief protectors, their mothers, are increasingly devalued in cultures around our world. Women too are increasingly likely to suffer as victims in modern warfare, all of which speaks deeply to the rejection of women and the devaluing of the spirit of the feminine and the mother image. If we can accept that our church authority is out of balance with the feminine principle of compassion and life-nurturing love due to its "all maleness" (i.e. women are not permitted to be ordained priests), can we also see this same imbalance writ large within civil government?

Most of the top-level political and economic decisions that create war are the domain of men. If we look at who is on the front lines of international military policy decisions in the United States, Afghanistan, Iraq, Pakistan and the Middle East, the majority are not only men, but lifelong military, the very people trained to give the orders to kill.

In this mix, the deep power of the feminine that Jesus so epitomized is crucified again. Paradoxically, this spirit of authentic womanhood could be a saving grace, the indispensable voice of nurturing maternal love, offsetting the all-male power structure's aggressive tendencies to rush and take up arms to protect.

THE VALUE OF THE FEMININE

The perfect yin/yang balance of male and female speaks very powerfully to our God image in Christianity. While Jesus is the fully developed male prophet, He exemplifies and evangelizes values we associate with the feminine—life-giving, healing, and merciful nonviolence. Jesus clearly valued women in an extremely patriarchal world of People Israel. Whether it was the Samaritan woman at the well (John 4:4), the central importance of Mary the Mother of God in the life of Jesus and the Church or his appearing to Mary Magdalene after his death (John 20:16), women are consistently soul mates to Jesus. They appear throughout the Gospels as people of major significance. Is there any real wonder that in this overly masculine world of church and state, where women are too often absent in the decision-making processes, we humans have become so quick with the sword? Doesn't it follow that the church in this wounded and imbalanced condition is quick to bless wars of the state while failing in their duty to protect children from abuse?

The present crisis of sexual abuse by priests has produced within Christendom and civil society an historic opportunity. The Catholic Church is now forced to look deeply into its medieval hierarchical governance, its all-male priesthood, including the vow of celibacy and the role of women and laity. If we can courageously look at ourselves, boldly confront sexual abuse and the self-defeating imperfections in church governance, won't such self-scrutiny create a more just and non-dominative, gender balanced way of being Church? Won't the kind of Church that evolves certainly remind us more of Jesus? Won't this Church be a true "Peace Church"?

This is the Church of Nonviolent Love that will continually inspire us to turn from justified, "theologically correct" violence, to a condemnation of every bomb, every gun, and every naval ship, no matter who owns them in the name of the God of Love? This will be a Church that protects the vulnerable child in all cultures. Are we ready as a church for the Spirit of the Divine Feminine to be in balance with the established God as Father, so that our God image and experience speak to all the faithful with the Christ-like force of truth and love?

Care of children as a first priority will be a reality only when the faithful worship and follow a God who expresses both mother/father, nurturer of all life. This God image embodies traits of masculine: a prophetic risk-taking for truth with full knowledge of the life threatening consequences. Our God also mirrors the feminine: maternal caring, with love that is long suffering, unconditional and grounded in the primacy of Christ-like mercy. It is now a *kairos* time for the church and for the people of God to move out of the prison of domination into the abode of protective love, even for the lives of the children of the enemy.

Jesus leaves us with a command: "Love one another as I have loved you." (Jn: 15; 12) Jesus, who embodies this prophetic balance of masculine and feminine, lives and dies in the embrace of Divine Mercy. The good news is that He will join us as we risk transforming our egos for the sake of this love, as Jesus asserts: "Lo, I am with you always, even to the close of the age." (Matt 28:20)

16

Living a Harmless Life

MOST OF US WATCH war from the sidelines. Of the ten billion humans who have lived over hundreds of thousands of years, a vast majority has never been directly engaged in taking another's life. Some of these bystanders are serious observers, as warfare is, after all, a dark fascination, a kill-or-be-killed drama that runs the entire course of history. Poems have been written and endless movies have been produced chronicling the great battles of history's great wars. Tolstoy, a veteran of the military, wrote, "War has always interested me, not war in the sense of maneuvers devised by great generals, but the reality of war, the actual killing . . . and in what way and under the influence of what feelings one soldier kills another."[126]

If we keep the power of observation going, we can also ask just what creates the climate that makes war so consistently possible and who puts the soldiers up to the killing that so struck Tolstoy? The "good wars" in history were fought to protect the homeland. Yet, even those who thought they fought nobly had a curious and telling word for their experience: "Hell." This metaphor depicts being trapped in the worst living nightmare of pain one could have in this life. But inside Hell or out, fight and protect we must, and war has continued to march through history.

Then the 20th Century and the Wars to End War. In this century of conflagration, homicidal panic stretched across Europe and Asia and engulfed the world. In 1961, in the aftermath of the bloodiest of all wars, came one of modern history's greatest warnings. President Dwight D.

Eisenhower, former general and war hero of "The Great War," spoke with uncharacteristic passion about the dark cloud that hovered over the U.S. during the cold war -"The Military Industrial Complex."[127] This juggernaut, consisting of the executive branch of government working in concert with the arms industry corporations and the military, was now leading the U.S. into a new, even more dangerous era. Warfare would not only be the necessary force protecting our national security, but war itself and the selling of weaponry, were becoming the most profitable of transactions between nations. The U.S. came out of World War I, a contending world economic and military power and we solidified that power after leading the allies to victory in World War II.

Heading into the cold war, the U.S. discovered new rationales for a strong military: (1.) Protect our newfound wealth and political power, and (2.) Increase that wealth and power by selling arms to any nation, friend or foe who could afford them. From the 1980's until the present, we have waged and won low-intensity wars, especially resource wars (i.e. protecting access to oil). To err on the side of waging a war also helps field tests and refine new weapons systems that posture our influence world-wide, perfecting our ability to position ourselves advantageously for present and future energy resources, especially oil.

A well-known fact unearths the human engine that drives U.S. wars since the 1990s: We are only 4% of the world's population controlling 50% of the world's resources and consuming 25% of the world's most available energy.[128] By 2035, U.S. demand for oil will jump from 25 million barrels today to 32 million barrels a day.

MATERIAL THINGS AND WAR

Because we consume not 4% but 50% of the world's resources, we live more or less in a perpetual state of frenzy—getting, spending, keeping, and protecting. In 1947, the average American spent $6,500 on material possessions, goods and services. Today, adjusted for inflation, we spend an average of over $14,000 per adult. We spend twice as much for a house three times as large and fill it with twice as many appliances, cars, clothes, computers, cell phones, and televisions. We work many more, exhausting hours."[129] Between 1973 and 2000, an average employee added 199 hours to their annual schedule, the equivalent of five forty-hour weeks.[130]

Our addiction to this getting and spending, though seemingly irrational, ferociously directs and controls the engines of the global economy. One of the fears our political leaders play on so masterfully to the privileged classes, is the fear of the loss of material power that threatens our self-ordained entitlement to climb and command the economic class ladder. For most Americans, to lose our competitive edge is tantamount to an annihilation of our birthright, this inherent right to command the global economy and lead the world.

The advantage we prize so much is our unimpeded ability to consume. This largely unconscious desire to "have" speaks directly to our most human dilemma, the fact that we *must* buy and consume in order to survive. But it is precisely in buying things that we strengthen forces of addictive habit. We've developed an insatiable pattern of materialist living that looks to money to fulfill our deepest security needs. In 1985, only 1.3% of the people born in 1910 had had a major depressive episode in their lifetimes. In contrast, the study found that those born after 1960 had a 5.3 percent chance of a major depressive episode, even though they had lived no longer than twenty five years.[131] A so-called healthy and rapidly growing economy post World War II, hasn't produced an increased percentage of healthy or happy people. Our new "gilded age" is now a gilded cage.

The visionary economist E.F. Schumacher warns in *Small is Beautiful:* "The cultivation and expansion of needs is the antithesis of wisdom. It is also the antithesis of freedom and peace. Every increase of need tends to increase our dependence on outside forces over which one cannot have control and therefore increases existential fear."[132] With this "faith" in wealth, our self-understanding and the sense of security that goes with it are now under the control of forces over which we have absolutely no control.

WEALTH AND RIVALRY

We as humans are tied into everything around us and are born into a particular way of interacting with each other. We simply are not born autonomous beings, learning life from scratch. We mimic what we see, and are therefore deeply conditioned by the mores and habits of the environments in which we grow.

French Theologian Rene Girard illuminates this in his seminal work *Violence and the Sacred:* "All the grown-up voices around (us) beginning with those of the father and mother . . . speak for the culture with the force of established authority exclaiming . . . imitate me; I bear the secret of life of true being. The more attentive the child is to these seductive words, the more earnestly he/she responds to suggestions emanating from all sides. (However), the child possesses no perspective that will allow them to see things as they are." We have imitated the message "you are what you have."[133]

We are conditioned with total completeness, to value consumption of goods over quality of relationships, and we imbibe this value from parents on forward into every walk of life. In our culture, the "bottom line" has become a metaphorical expression for what is really important. The origin of the term of course refers to money; for, in the end, you add up the numbers and either you have it or you do without.

The value of money is most visible in the economics of the family. How many people have told me over the past twenty years that a family can survive financially only if both parents work, full time if possible? Now parents must hire others to help raise their children. A dominant idiom of our modern middle class suburban world, "keeping up with the Joneses" is precisely the economic treadmill that these families are treading on. Coveting our neighbors' goods, a ten-commandment stricture, is one of the central seductions that conditions the collective mind in American culture.

Girard speaks to this foundational drive to possess, naming it "mimetic (mimic) desire" that propels all humans into perpetual rivalry. "The rival desires the same object as the subject (the dominant one in the rivalry); in desiring the object, the rival alerts the subject to the desirability of the object. Once (our) basic needs are satisfied, (we) are subject to intense desires though they may not be precisely known . . . The reason is that (we) desire 'being', that (the rival) him/herself lacks, and some other person seems to possess (the dominant one in the rivalry)." The rival looks to the other to inform them of what they should acquire in order to have 'that' being."[134] And when the rivalry clashes over power and dominance, we have violence.

When we find ourselves desperately wanting what someone else has, we yearn for fulfillment, for true being in gaining this possession. The dominant one (the U.S.) may start out on a pedestal but the rivalry born of envy often deteriorates into the law of the jungle. We desperately seek what is outside of us. We will even sacrifice our freedom in the contest, chasing the object, which, in contemporary terms, is money and the things money can buy.

In a frantic attempt to keep up with the Joneses, instead following a true calling to authentic being, we follow what is separate and alien to our deepest selves—wealth, possessions, status, competition, and eventually the violence that procures and protects it. Such a frustrated purpose, profound insecurity, and subservience to the dominant authority, become the fruits of perpetual rivalry.

It is fundamentally true that "violence is always mingled with desire."[135] It is not a great leap from frustrated subservience to anxiety to a vicious circle of reciprocal violence to then fighting for your "life." Our inner lives harbor these seeds of warrior violence. We sow them with our aggressive patriotic rhetoric even as we observe this same compulsion in the bully pulpit of those who send the young off to war, and in the zealous warriors themselves.

WHAT DO WE REALLY NEED?

The Joneses are rugged individualists in a tightly bound and protected nuclear family construct. For our family to stay in a rivalry with them, we urgently need work; not necessarily meaningful work, but work that pays for the ever-increasing competitive material desires. This attitude toward work can keep us in a perpetually unfulfilled state, charging up the ladders of success with increasing desires and needs. Driven to compete, we are propelled to get and spend. But in this tandem of "get and spend" we must first "get" and then work will make us the money to spend.

In 1959, my sixth grade teacher told me, "Brayton, by the time you are an adult, you will need a graduate degree just to get a job." Here is a microcosmic moment in which we have the whole economic scenario forecasted. First, an elder teacher tells a child about life in the adult world and imparts to the student a most serious reality: resources in the future will be scarcer than in the present. We know as competitors that not everyone will be in a position to earn a graduate degree, so you, Brayton, had better get one. This privilege will give you a chance not just to survive but also to stay competitive, and therefore "happy." Rivalry begins young.

Our political contests play on this fear of scarcity. At some point in every campaign, we hear each candidate plead, "Vote for me and I will create more *jobs.*" Fears based on money-driven anxiety, lie at the heart of rivalry, and it easily manipulated by politicians as they pitch "a good economy is a growth economy with more and more *jobs.*"

What is never asked in the "job" equation is: "What does just 'any utilitarian work' do to the worker?" The *quality* of work is never mentioned. Money consistently overshadows the meaning we need to find in our work.

The collective expression of this competitive pride is our sense of patriotism. "I live in a good, hardworking, prosperous country. We've earned this privileged status with good, honest, hard work." An unstated assumption about the world we live in is that everyone cannot have equal access to wealth. Therefore, undocumented immigrants are not welcome in the U.S. where they compete for limited resources, which drives more rivalry.

Schumacher recounts an article in the *London Times* describing most work in an industrial society: "Dante, when composing his visions of hell, might well have included the mindless, repetitive boredom of working on a factory assembly line. It destroys initiative and rots brains, yet millions of British workers are committed to it for most of their lives." Schumacher marvels that "This statement, like countless others made before it, aroused no interest; there were no hot denials or anguished agreements; no reactions at all. These visions of hell attracted no reprimand that they were misstatements or overstatements, irresponsible, hysterical exaggerations or subversive propaganda; no, people read them, sighed and nodded, I suppose, and moved on."[136]

Therefore, for many, to be promised jobs is to be promised life sentences of meaningless doing in a beast of burden slavery to some variation of the assembly line. Centuries of unchecked industrial capitalism have deadened the human desire for meaningful labor for the company laborer. We simply have come to accept that there will be no essential meaning in most career jobs.

Work in this context even for most worker owners is a sacrifice of our freedom to create, our happiness and satisfaction, our most vital waking hours in exchange for economic security, a most bitter but necessary pill if we truly want to possess what others have and wish to measure our true being by satisfying our wants. Our self-alienation is simple—we work too much for too many years for the wrong reward. Mammon becomes the true, yet tragic God. And the Gods of war are always ready and willing to defend the God of Money. Our contemporary lifestyles are now book ended with a sad blend of self-inflicted violence: "War is hell. Our bread jobs are hell."

GETTING OFF THE TREADMILL

Jesus' teaching on Divine Providence drives a wedge into the center of the question of security: "You cannot serve two masters—God and money." What we "worship" makes the fruits of our lives visible. Jesus also has a very low opinion of the worry about getting enough: "Therefore I tell you do not be anxious about your life, what you shall eat or drink, nor about your body what you shall wear, is not life more than food . . . the body more than clothing." (Matt 6: 24–34) This most countercultural of all Jesus' teachings can only be heard if we are aware of which societal forces have conditioned our thinking and behavior to this point; that is, a fixation on economic insecurity propelling us into a frenzied hoarding and consumption.

Jesus' gospel message doesn't so much give us an economic program for simple living, as it urges us to renounce the habitual worry about our own material well-being. What is the financial plan that replaces economic privilege where too much is never enough? "Seek ye first the kingdom of God and all things (necessary) will be given unto you." (Matt 6:33) Do not lay up treasures for *yourself*. The corollary? Do not count the cost when spending your "wealth" on the ways of God.

If the Divine Plan is a gift of life for us to love, wouldn't that Divine Plan include enough to survive on? If "life" is more than food and material possessions, then the life-force and this teaching have a direct line to the Eternal. In the effort to be faithful to this trust in Divine Providence, Jesus doesn't disparage work. Work is among the most human and necessary endeavors. St. Paul draws a connection between the need to work and the claim to deserve the right to eat. That is the social contract. We contribute our labor, and "the laborers deserve their wages." (1 Tim 5:18)

One of the most persistent fallacies that shapes our self-image is "We are what we do." We will not overcome our insecurity fears with a job; we will not discover our true selves by some act of doing. The question is: "In what spirit do I work. How much work is too much work? How much money is too much money?" Jesus instructs again: "Don't worry about tomorrow." (Matt 6:34) His teaching on economics is not so much "Money is evil", but rather "Don't think so often about money," don't hoard it for tomorrow, don't make wealth a warlike force of anxious rivalry, and this will free you up to serve the urgent needs of those in your midst today.

This teaching has helped us at the Agape community to remain focused on ministry dedicated to others and not consumed with fretting about revenue and the needs of the community. Reaching out to poor families in town, relating to those in prison, protesting war, offering hospitality, raising children and caring for children at risk all are efforts that transform us, backing us away from "the works of war," and an over-focus on money earned, money spent. These principles remain the heartbeat of community life. Non-revenue generating work activities often meet the greatest need and bring the greatest human satisfaction as they are a necessary way of slowing down the modern fixation of keeping the engines of bread labor and commerce in a perpetual grind. Modern economics, i.e. money "in", defines major activities of the modern world and is the idol of livelihood that compromises the art of living for God.

"Right livelihood," central to Buddha's vision of the eight-fold path, is powerfully instructive. How can we allow our spiritual values to define our livelihood? How can we make a living that fosters nonviolent love of all people and protection of God's green earth? Can we demand that our work life be both necessary *and* creative, serve the common good, not the ego and satisfy the deepest human longing, namely, to be engaged in meaningful, productive labor that will define the majority of our waking hours throughout our most productive years?

Is there any better wealth than living for life itself? May this celebration of a simpler, nonviolent life, our commitment to a "right livelihood," truly end the need for all wars of protection for all time?

SECTION V

Peace with the Earth

17

Deep Green of the Divine

GROWING UP IN SUBURBAN America, the image of God I most frequently encountered was that of a white male. I've concluded since that time, that this was a projected God image of the wealthy class of primarily Caucasian men who ruled my world. So often in this world, women, people of color and the poor are devalued and have no significant stature.

As Christianity developed into the modern era in the West, the image of Jesus became increasingly that of a white, blue-eyed Messiah who could comfortably project the face and the inner world of male-driven empire, a God who made the dominant European economic values more acceptable. Echoing ancient parallels alongside People Israel's Divine Right of Kings, whereby the Jew's king was an agent of God and the power of Kingship was a Divine power; patriarchy was handed down through history.

God continues to be represented as male, sufficing as a perfect symbol for the European Imperial King and his empire. Order in Empire is achieved by war; plundering the earth provides wealth and subjugating the masses of the poor keeps wealth where it belongs.

America inherited a "God" made in a Caucasian image and likeness, so simpatico was it with empire and a vision of world dominance. Our "kings and presidents" and our manifest destiny schemes of empire became the elect of God. After all, some country has to run the world and control all. It appears God has chosen us.

As we move through the early 21st century, Christianity and other western cultural and religious traditions are experiencing a profound, almost continual moral and spiritual turmoil, decay and transition. In that volatility, the color shade of the Divine is evolving from white male to verdant deep green. The one true God is increasingly associated with the creation story of Genesis, where we meet the God and creator of all life whose primary color is green that shade of earth that represents natural things. Life is loved into existence in its fullest spectrum, not just humans, rich and poor, oppressed and free, but all that lives and shares its existence on our fragile planet.

Because we humans are the only mammals who sleep on our backs, we are positioned well to gaze into the night sky, where we can "see" beyond our anthropocentrism; our thinking that humans and their needs are the first and most valid priority among all that lives on Earth. When human need alone becomes paramount, we descend into fighting each other over the resources of the earth and otherwise plunder "her" to gain our advantages. Thomas Aquinas observes: "The whole universe together participates in the Divine Goodness more perfectly and represents it better than any single creature whatsoever."[137]

Anthropocentrism, that *humans and their needs are the highest good in all existence,* is an anthropology we have inherited since the first Homo sapiens inhabited this earth. That humans dominate the created order lends itself well to a male dominating hierarchical world view. But as we evolve our thinking and move toward a more dynamic balance with the feminine in a vulnerable, gentle, and life-affirming way, we move closer to the deep green of the Divine. "Male and female, God created them, all of the animals and plants in the sea and on land, God created them." (Gen 1:27) What was wanting in one was supplied by the other.

"God saw all God had made and indeed it was very good," continues the first chapter of Genesis. The first passage in the Bible points to the foundational reality of life. God's goodness is re-created in all of life. Because God saw God's creation as "good," it has an indelible mark of the sacred. Harm brought to *any of creation* is sacrilege, a violation against life and its inherent goodness, conferred by God. Because humans are made in God's image, that is, in love, we humans are to exercise the virtue of loving kindness toward all that lives.

We must not exploit the earth or harm it for our own ends, to gain advantage over weaker humans while dominating other forms of life. God grants human beings a privileged role as stewards of creation, to have "dominion" over the earth and its creatures. But, the Divine gives us dominion only in solemn trust to uphold responsibly the sanctity of life in all its forms. It is the only spirit of dominion that Jesus offers us, that of "suffering servant" in shared stewardship, sustainers of life.

HEBREW SCRIPTURES AND THE SACRED

The Hebrew word for humankind, "Adam" is derived from the word for earth, "Adama," harkening back to Genesis and the origins of life. "For dust you are and to dust you shall return." (Gen. 3:19) Only humans in their non-dominating humility (from humus, the soil) can see that they are "of the earth."

The oneness of humanity with all earth's creatures is the central image of the flood. In the disaster of the flood, humans are called to be stewards and protectors of all other species as Noah was. The picture of all earth's animals crowded together in extremity and interdependent, symbolizes the inherent message willed by a loving God: we will all struggle and survive *together*. God doesn't abandon us even in life-threatening catastrophe. "Behold I establish my covenant with you . . . and with every living creature." (Gen. 9:9–11) This is hardly a mandate for male hierarchy, human greed and exploitation of the earth, for human survival only. At creation, God addresses the animals first before humans.

God has given us "dominion over the earth," which should not be confused with domination. Hebrew Scripture Scholar Claus Westermann writes of the foundational Hebrew idea of "*nefresh nayya*," that humans are bound together with beasts, birds, fishes, and insects. Dominion, according to Westermann's research, "Does not even include the right to kill animals for food. Since the priestly creation story and Yahwehist account in the second chapter of Genesis portray humans as vegetarians eating the fruits and plants and trees for their food. People would forfeit their principal role among the living, were the animals made the object of their whim."[138]

The Hebrew Scriptures continually characterize the oneness of all creatures in the same unity of *nefresh nayya*. It is important to note that ancient Hebrew cultures had no word for "nature" because they didn't as humans see themselves apart from the natural world. Humans in their profound need were to stand with all of creation in utter dependence on God. These archetypal Hebrew Scriptures and inspired writings hold up the sacredness of all life, the story of our human origins and the unified whole of all the earth's species, plants, animals, air, earth, and soil. That life is sacred is not a cliché, but a warning.

To proclaim the greenness of the Judeo-Christian tradition, we don't need to have a reformed foundation document or to make up a new one. We simply need to read with new eyes the Hebrew Scriptures, the Genesis story, Job, the prophets, the Psalms into the New Testament, to find where God continually demonstrates deep concern *for all creation*.

JESUS AND THE NEW TESTAMENT

The gospel writers portray Jesus as a prophet who communes with wild beasts and stills a storm. Birthed within the rigorous natural elements of a stable surrounded by animals, he spent a great deal of his life outdoors, worked simply with his hands and wits as a carpenter, building with natural materials. He rubbed shoulders with shepherds, fishermen and farmers. The influence that "nature wisdom" had on him was quite obvious in his preaching exemplified by the Parable of the Sower in the gospels.

Using the common experience of watching how plants grow, the parable symbolically teaches us the realities of the human condition. By observing what nurtures or inhibits plants that are sown from seed, Jesus teaches his faithful the essential wisdom about how to grasp and live the word of God.

Even Jesus' Resurrection impacts the earth's natural rhythms—the day goes dark and the great earthquake rocks the very foundations of the Earth. This Prophet Messiah's message always came from the everyday existence of living "close to the land." He was born into an understanding and love of the essential rhythms of the earth and taught from that vantage point. His life, his message, and his earth-connected world guide us profoundly in these urgent times of ecological crisis.

PAGANS AND NATURE SPIRITS

The pagan people in cultures before Judaism believed on one level, in a multiplicity of divinities located inside or associated with the various forms of nature—streams, trees, earth, air, and mountains. The new and radical monotheism that became Judaism was prone to a rigid interpretation of "one God over all." This theology began to cancel the idea that the spirit world could any longer exist within the natural world. Some of these first monotheists with their dim view of pagans unwittingly ushered in the beginnings of nature denuded of all mystique and sanctity. Robbed of her intrinsic sacredness, nature was now in harm's way. Her world could more easily become de-sacralized, treated like a thing, or worse, seen as "lower or profane." The spirit world of nature no longer was a protection from the anxiety and greed of humans.

Another uniquely human force threatened the beauty and spiritual power of the natural world—humans' fear of scarcity. The question has always loomed large in human cultures throughout millennia: "Is there enough sustenance on the earth for all humans to survive?" The Biblical answer throughout history is definitive: "Yes. God will provide." Life is so abundant that we can afford to take a Sabbath Day once a week, inspired by God's rest. God observed the seventh day of creation. (Gen. 2:2) Hebrews survived fear of famine in the desert of Egypt due to God's enduring provisions of superabundance. We need not fear the destitution of scarcity, and as long as the people gathered only what they needed, there was "never a shortage." (Ex. 16:18)

Ancient Israel was learning an economic lesson that still stares us squarely in the face. The superabundance of life which flows from a generous God is a Gospel truth, speaking of Divine Providence, a force that can reverse fear of scarcity and guide us with a steady hand as we all struggle for the life-sustaining provisions of everyday existence. (Matthew 6:25–34)

No, we needn't hoard nor fight over the lucre, the necessities of this life nor land. But one sacred law must rule. To know this sacred law, that a generous God provides superabundantly, we must not take more than our basic human needs dictate. An ultimate responsibility comes with being stewards of this fecund and fertile earth, a teaching that comes straight from Jesus. *Who in this world is in need of basic survival? Who is suffering want due to our hoarding and our fear of scarcity? How can we alter our living habits to respond to a plundered earth and her starving masses?* To maintain the sanctity of life, it is paramount to look beyond ourselves.

PROPERTY AND OWNERSHIP

Nowhere does the demon of scarcity control us as it does with property and the right to own, control, and develop it. Our golden calf of private property has devastating effects on our environment. But ancient lore has a different story. The ancient Hebrew laws discouraged the faithful from "owning property" with a simple premise: God is the overseer of all the earth: "The land shall not be sold in perpetuity the Lord told Moses on Mt. Sinai, for the land is mine for you are strangers and sojourners with me."(Lev. 25:23) In concert with this teaching, the prophet Micah warns: "Woe to those who devise wickedness. They covet fields and seize them." (Micah 2: 1–2) We have traveled a very different road since the warnings of the Hebrew Prophets.

Property law and rights in the U.S. were inherited from the Common Law of England, but as the U.S. developed and became a major nation-state, property lines were intensified to reflect the extremes of individualism that mirrored this new American frontier spirit. Our Founding Fathers, especially Jefferson, perceived property as an essential right because it allowed adult white males to make a living working the land. At the same time, Jefferson was troubled by the fact that people of means owned land at the expense of the poor. The right to "develop land," that is, to do with your land what you want, in American Property Law came increasingly to reflect our nation's individualistic culture and in so doing rejected our English origin which respected the common good over the private good.

No legal development would highlight the resulting differences more significantly than Britain's Town and Country Planning Act, enacted right after WWII. As American law was entrenching the landowner's inherent right to develop, British law was largely taking it away. British law emphasized that development had to contain a comparable benefit to the public. Property was not first and foremost an individual right. It began with the understanding of the common good. British landowners thereafter could build on their lands only with prior government approval.

Throughout the 19th century in the United States, the force of the "Do No Harm" rule of land ownership began to lessen and to accommodate itself to environmental demands of the burgeoning Industrial Revolution. The noisier, dirtier activities of this Industrial age joined with the rise of Capitalism. During these last earth-shattering centuries, Americans have progressively forgotten the essential links between property rights and health of the environment, rewriting property law to stimulate the ecologically savaging growth of the corporation.

A tragic history began-of over-fishing, of deadly mining operations and of privatized water rights. Eventually, property law in its agrarian form posed too much of a roadblock for industrial growth. [139] Up to the present, we continue to suffer from this human mindset, motivated both by the fear of the common good (scarcity) and a possessive sense of private property as a personal right for financial gain (scarcity again).

All but lost is a sense of the sacred, that land is a gift of God to be loved, sustained, and shared according to the needs of humans other than ourselves as well as of animals and plants that inhabit this vulnerable earth with us. If we humans wish to survive into this next millennium, we must radically and urgently learn new ways of living in harmony with the earth while upholding the sanctity of all life. In our attempts to discover sustainable ways of being on the earth, we must seek to invest in the fullness of life by giving back to the earth and her life forms more than we take from them.

Such a spiritual revolution will celebrate and strengthen the sacred circle of all life on this threatened planet. As Christians of the 21st century, can we join in this Spirit Earth Revolution? Can we love God and follow Jesus by revering and sustaining the earth that our Deep Green and Loving God has so created?

18

Building the Circle

CONSTRUCTION OF OUR STRAW bale house, Brigid House, began in 1990, as we were captured by the allure of building something that inspires us to live in harmony with the earth. For all modern history, most humans have lived in a domicile of some kind, but in so doing, questions remain: What kind of house? Built with what inspiration? Is this house we live in kind to our natural environment?

As our culture continues to live in and through this green revolution, we are reminded that in our current world more than ever we are presented with a choice—either progress toward a sustainable and simpler way of living or hand today's young generations an unlivable planet. We are joining others with this same desire for a healthy, peace-filled life that places us in deep accord, not only among humans but also within the embrace of all life.

Inspired by that vision, we at Agape have endeavored to reject any notion of a triumph of technology over nature, and to return to a more elemental pattern of a wholesome, physically hard working, non-injurious way of being. To learn an art and science of sustainable living, one must take the primary cue from nature herself, to mimic her ways (she never rushes nor hoards), to live and flourish within her sacred and regenerative circle. The more hearty and ecologically sound this circle, the more minimal will be the waste byproducts that clog and poison the environment.

We also live and build as 21st Century Christians. Environmentalist and theologian, Sallie McFague, writes in *Super Natural Christians*: "Christianity had better get on the environmental bandwagon because commitment to the God of Jesus Christ demands it. Christian nature spirituality is the logical next step from a tribal God, away from a God concerned with me and my kind toward the One concerned with the entire creation."[140]

Our way of life needs this "design." How we want to exist in this world must be a plan, a sacred logic that permits life-enhancing patterns to emerge and flourish while it simultaneously discourages life-destroying patterns. To design from a conviction to live out environmentally sustainable methods in the 21st century can have a deep effect on the way a community such as Agape conceives designs and builds a house.

THE FIRST CIRCLE—BUILDING WITH STRAW

After the delivery to our homestead of 300 straw bales to build a 2,500 square foot, three bedroom straw bale house, the children and the animals excitedly and immediately made a home in them. Saturated with the smell of earth and field, this "wheaty" aroma translated -*life*. Having a deep trust in what they love to play in, children consistently appropriated our bales as a golden castle nested in with their pets.

Within weeks, the stacks of bales became actual walls of the house, the very image of earth connectedness and balance. A healthy balance is maintained in nature when all that grows lives within a regenerative circle. Straw cut from grain is a yearly renewable resource, with no need to clear-cut forests in order to build with its wood; and instead of burning straw as garbage, many of us are learning to build sturdy walls with it. Our national grain yield produces over 200 million tons of straw each year, from wheat, barley, oats, rice, rye, and flax, enough straw to build five million, 2,000 square foot homes each year at half the cost of conventional building.[141]

To live within the sacred loop that sustains, we must always ask: how much energy, especially heating and cooling with oil and gas will the building require each year? Even in the world of green building, straw bale construction rates first in energy conservation. At R-50, straw has twice the heat energy conservation rating of the most current conventionally built super insulated houses.[142] Infusing the senses with the aromas of the farm, the builders regretted the thought of having to cover the beautiful sight and smell of straw with earthen plaster to finish the inside walls.

In choosing to complete the framing of the house with post and beam construction, we selectively cut oak and maple trees from Agape's 34 acres and hired a logger to drag the logs quietly in with his team, two majestic Clydesdale horses, without burning any oil. The logs were immediately milled on site for the posts and beams, and the resulting boards were used for flooring and the bark and scraps burned for heat. Another circle is maintained.

Throughout North America, we "European Settlers" have been formed by the nature-spirituality influence of native peoples and traditions which reverentially use *all* plant or animal we kill without exploitation or waste and to always endeavor to return back to the natural world more than we take. For most of us, the circle idea started with Indian Nations.

It is difficult to list even one unpleasant factor in building with straw, except perhaps the ongoing, tirelessly awful "Three Little Pigs" jokes. But what a straw building does for the imagination is magical as much as mystical; and it is certainly worth persevering through this continuous monotonous humor. When explaining straw bale construction to a newcomer, we have come to almost hear the wheels of the skeptic's mind grinding toward . . . convinced!

THE CIRCLE EXTENDS—FLUSHING WITHOUT WATER?

The ecological loop we that we live within at Agape originates with the phototropic power of the sun, fueling the growth of the trees, our primary lifestyle resource for heat energy and building which culminates in ash from our woodstove. When this ash fertilizes the soil of our food supply, our circle widens with the question: How do we dispose of human waste?

The answer: We built a compost toilet to collect and utilize human waste. When we perfectly mimic the rhythms of nature there is zero waste; waste of one set of creatures can be food, fertilizer, or habitat for another. The compost toilet applies and integrates lessons learned from nature. Refuse from what we consume as humans is not discarded as waste and simply considered useless. Rather our composted "waste" becomes a resource to be managed and utilized within a regenerative circle that sustains our growing soil.

As long as water goes down and out, who needs to care about the rest? "Out of mind" systems tend to be environmentally costly as well. Did we know that 40% of all residential drinking water is consumed by flush toilets?[143] To what end? Most septic systems can potentially pollute ground water. Full of toxic chemicals and nitrites, sewer systems are the primary threat to North America's most polluted bio-systems—our lakes and rivers. The amount of water Americans use daily considering water used in products consumed, irrigation, washing, and drinking is 1,565 gallons per person per day. It takes

2,000 tons of water to flush one ton of human waste, 40% of our drinking water. We are depleting 21 billion gallons of ground water each day.[144] These facts point directly to the myriad reasons for a compost toilet:

(1.) If built correctly it will not pollute groundwater. (2.) It conserves our gradually disappearing drinking water. (3.) The site-built compost privy's low-tech ingenuity minimizes specialized maintenance and energy consumption and costs about one tenth of the average flush toilet system to build and maintain. As with most of our methods of simplicity, the energy spent leans towards physical human effort along with building ingenuity and patience. (4.) This waste disposal system recycles waste with a de-composition process much like what happens naturally with leaves dying into a forest floor. And anything that "recycles" continues life in a circle of renewal not relegating it to the dead end "dump." (5.) Finally and most mi-raculously, after seven years of composting, the fertilized and transformed "waste" provides nutrients for our fruit trees and flower gardens, without pollutants or significant greenhouse gases. The circle is completed. Com-post toilets—they are the way to "go."

SOLAR—ORIGINATES THE CIRCLE OF LIFE

The average house is ablaze with a million lights. Each lamp looks innocent enough, but Steve Kurkoski, our solar energy contractor, shared with us an uneasy fact. "Every time we plug something into an electrical outlet and light the bulb, we trash the earth." Why? To drive grid electricity, some oil, propane, and coal must be burned to fuel their generators. Of all building issues, massive, non-sustainable energy use most indicts our first world habits of living. There is a Saudi saying: "My father rode a camel. I drive a car. My son flies a jet airplane. His son will ride a camel." This return to so called "primitive ways" will become more necessary even in North America, and sooner than we think.

In the fall of 2012, we at Agape completed our five-year plan to wean ourselves off all fossil fuels for household use through generous donations from our extended community. Questions still remain in our journey towards conserving our resources: How many lights do we need? Two? Three? Ten? Fifty? How many watts per bulb are needed to see in the dark? How many gadgets- a DVD player, a computer in every room, phones ring-ing everywhere? How do we pump a running water system that is "green" from our well? And how will we heat water and refrigerate food? All these "conveniences" require fossil fuel and grid-driven electricity (more fossil fuel), and year by year makes the American lifestyle an all-consuming, financially expensive, carbon spewing, Wal-Mart purchased, un-recycled garbage dump waiting to happen.

As we look to our immediate future, we look at how we live and ask: Do we need to break with the recent past and return to the distant past doing everything by hand, Amish style—the primary energy source being sweat, muscle, building skill and patience to learn environmentally sound and slower ways of living? Or can we supplement their simple, wholesome, hard, hand-hewn way of life with something more modern?

At Agape, we attempted the latter by installing a solar driven energy system. This enables us to live off the sun, a non-toxic energy source that also allows us to live more photo tropically, honoring the fact that humans are sun-requiring beings with a biological need for sunlight. Add to this fact that without the sun's heat and light, there would be no life anywhere.

To run our lights and fans sparingly and pump water from the well, we enjoy an abundance of untapped low-carbon energy from the all- powering solar. We harness energy of stored sunlight in batteries monitored by a voltage regulator that warns of waning energy capacity. Because stored sunlight is not limitless electrical energy, conservation becomes the fundamental discipline of the solar energy user. Carelessly leave a light on and you jeopardize tomorrow's energy—no sun stored plus no practice of daily conservation equals no available power.

If we listen and watch, the earth's bio-systems communicate to us a need for our self-regulating conservation. Photovoltaic energy provides sunlight energy only as God's precious gift, unlike what our conventional electrical outlet seems to provide—plug it in and we are treated to an illusion of limitless energy, yet we are trashing the earth over and over. So where is an incentive to cut back on energy consumption? We live with a false impression of unrestricted supplies of affordable energy with no observable environmental crisis, an addictive illusion fostered by dangerously short memories of the recent BP Oil spill in the Gulf of Mexico and the extreme hurricanes of Katrina, Irene and Sandy, massive floods in Iowa and catastrophic draughts across the country

Our community has recently added solar hot water systems, placing a new array of solar panels on each community house rooftop. These hot water systems trap thermal heat from the sun, unlike solar electricity systems which convert sunlight into electricity. The sun's heat and light energy is free of charge, abundant, and does not create a single harmful byproduct or greenhouse gas emission, becoming a sustainable energy liberated from corporate-owned and controlled profit motives. But the real sticker price of this alternative energy is self-control. We must calm our addictive wants, modify our habits of dependency on environmentally toxic high technology and submit to the limits of earth's sacred boundaries.

CLOSING THE FOOD LOOP

Because earth has sacred value and because we are made in God's image, eating food of the earth is a sacred practice. Eating is also a bridge that unites human culture and survival with the earth as a verdant and fecund source of nourishment. It therefore requires a stewardship and spiritual care. To truly observe the natural world, minus the toxic human impact, we can see that it also functions instinctively within a regenerative circle. This is a vital instruction for how we humans are to grow and eat our food within this same pattern that recycles and replenishes the environment.

Eating, more than any other human activity binds us to nature. Today we have a growing awareness of how our eating habits can strengthen our own health and maintain the health of nature. To this end, we built our food generating laboratory that continues this food loop—a greenhouse. This body nourishing "temple" is symbolic of the choice we must make to heal our damaged system of food growing. The local greenhouse that connects to the local farm is the most environmentally urgent choice that we need to make to replace the corporate business of agriculture with its cancer-producing chemicals and pesticides.

Consider that at the time of the American Revolution, 98% of our population, including George Washington and Thomas Jefferson, had their roots in agriculture, and our population of farmers today is 2%.[145] We have subcontracted our food production and our health to a corporate food industry. Agribusiness flourishes because we depend on low nutrition, mass produced celery from Florida, oranges from California, peaches from Georgia, broccoli from Bolivia. Spewing the ozone with carbon dioxide, we ship in our food supply from far away bioregions securing it by drilling oil from foreign lands for its transport.

The average trip for the food we eat—1,300 miles.[146] This business of agriculture yields inefficient single-crop monoculture farms depleting the topsoil; 22% to 33% of climate change gases can be traced to our food system,[147] 18% to livestock.[148] An alarming example that the production of one pound of beef takes 4.5 gallons of oil[149] and 2,500 gallons of water to produce.[150] Another form of devastation is that this oil-drenched food supply creates an ongoing need for the U.S. to be quick to go to war to protect its heavy carbon footprint way of life—hence the Gulf War of 1991 and the invasions of Afghanistan (2001) and Iraq (2003).

Ever the agribusiness alternative, the local greenhouse is the agent of the local economy where we grow our seedlings and lettuce beds and learn the hard lessons of settling for what we can grow locally, taking Thoreau's advice seriously and "living in each season as it passes, breathing its air, tasting its fruit."[151]

Can we shift our food consumption over to the fruits and vegetables of Southern New England and away from Southern Latin America? Can we evolve our eating habits in the direction of a vegetarian diet to be more harmonious with our more plant eating digestive systems? We possess plant grinding teeth, not meat-ripping carnivorous cat-like teeth. We secrete digestive enzymes in our saliva and stomach that don't digest meat easily, especially the raw meat that carnivorous animals regularly eat. We have a liver and intestines that assimilate our food on a 24-hour cycle while typical carnivores eliminate in one to two hours of consuming their kill.[152]

The commercial food system in this country is undermining the health of the planet. A typical U.S. meat-eating diet generates nearly 1.5 tons more carbon dioxide per person per year than a plant based vegetarian diet.[153] Local, organic, plant based agriculture is the only real future we have with our earth.

With our greenhouses connecting to our gardens and the plant food we grow in them, we learn to bring food production back home where it has always traditionally been in the simpler and the more sustainable societies of our ancestors. World peace begins with living in each season as it passes, breathing its air tasting its fruit, partaking in these daily joys of homegrown, maintaining our ecological lives within the geographic boundaries and specific limitations of our particular bio-region that allows the local soil, climate, and topography to dictate what food we need to grow at what time of year.

pressing need to develop solar, wind, and geothermal energies that are the most earth friendly, and if widely used, would be economically affordable.

Wood's final destination is the main hearth's woodstove, that convivial gathering place that beckons us from the biting cold to the togetherness of warmth and a circle of conversation. In an effort to live more consciously, this culture of wood helps us participate directly in the production of heat energy by hand, locally and efficiently throughout very cold and demanding New England winters.

At the end of the cycle, we make one final run to our garden with the ashes from the burned logs, replenishing our soil with nitrogen. Much of the peace of Jesus is to be found in loving and walking lightly on this earth—"Give and it shall be given to you—good measure, pressed down, shaken together and running over." (Luke 6:38)

SECTION VI

Peace with the Soul

19

The Gift of Rest

AFTER 25 YEARS OF building community and a few years of planning and preparing, Suzanne and I began our sabbatical in October of 2007. With a commitment to stop our Agape work schedule, we included in that category all the programs, activities, gatherings, retreats, feast day celebrations, and daily hospitality. At first, I resisted the idea of letting go completely of these rich and varied moments. But, as the fall unfolded with nothing to plan or prepare for, I found the gift of rest overtaking my sense of disappointment. Rest and the relaxed peace of rest made me aware of the first lesson I was to know about work: as much as work gives us purpose, it can also run us into the ground.

My life's work isn't just another activity; it is my primary task. My "good work" forms my identity. Most peace people don't have to be convinced to be responsible and diligent. We do need to be convinced to leave our work for rest and contemplation, aware that we are all reared in a work-addicted society driven by financial security fears.

In my case, I am known for the activities of Agape that I help plan and animate. From time to time, my activities gain some publicity in local newspapers. People become aware of me through my work. For example, we visited noted Franciscan Fr. Richard Rohr during our sabbatical. In an e-mail he said, "I have known of the good work of Agape for some time." Work may attract notoriety and appreciation. Then, there is the additional fact that I was educated primarily for gainful employment and to "make a living." So what happens to me when I quit, voluntarily, most, if not all the work of my community?

I AM NOT WHAT I DO

It took about a month or so of "closing up" the systems of Agape before we could say we were officially closed. It was a lengthy job, buttoning up twenty five years of work. Even then, I noticed the temptations to check e-mail and voicemail. I became aware of the first few trials of sabbatical at home—cues to work were persistently around me. Even if I could resist the temptation, my mind continually churned with still urgent tasks and unfinished business. I soon discovered that it is far easier to break with the routine of work if I leave the community itself. True rest is relaxing the mind, not the body, simply because most of us think about work or actually work compulsively all day long. I began to learn a fierce lesson: let all familiar work tasks go, including closing up the garden.

Similar to our weekly practice of Sabbath during community life, our "sabbatical at home" required constant mindfulness, consistently walking away from the temptation to finish grinding the herbs, fulfill social obligations, return phone calls and e-mails. Now I knew why, in the Jewish tradition of Sabbath, there are 39 prohibitions against working on the Sabbath. Sabbatical for me was becoming an extended Sabbath.

I took the first two months of our ten-month sabbatical on the community property, seeking refuge in the stillness of our hermitage tucked away a few hundred yards behind Francis House, our main residence. It soon became clear to me that I wished the silence of retreat to be the main activity of my sabbatical. As Suzanne and I planned our new way of being, exploring the world and vacationing rest would not be our entire time. But as co-workers and founders who live in community, our Sabbatical time included time together in silence, in enjoyment or celebration, and time away from each other. As a first-generation lay community person blazing a new trail with no strong history of daily spiritual practices or Sabbatical to inherit, perfect and look forward to, I find myself creating or adapting traditions as I need them.

While spending half of my days in almost complete wilderness silence in Agape's hermitage, two surprises emerge. First, I observe the chatter of the mind and a voice urging me: "Be more productive." This voice keeps asking: "Aren't you going to write to have something to show for all this?" My mind, like most people's minds is based on the progress model. We are drawn to produce, to perfect, and nothing I am accomplishing at the present moment is ever really good enough. Spending time meditating, reading Scripture and gazing out the window is not "progress" to this, my conditioned mind. For two months, I spent each full morning from sunrise to lunch, in or around the hermitage, with this voice, urging productivity, as a daily companion.

The second experience was silence. Of all the mysteries of faith, silence is the hardest to explain. Thoreau wrote about this mystery: "Silence doesn't translate well into English." The calling I felt to silence was the counter voice to this voice of productivity. To stop working and sit in silence immediately clashed with the daily drive to produce. We not only live in a speed-driven and acquisitive culture, but the most frantic and acquisitive in history.

The cultural air we breathe keeps us busy with more, whetting the appetite for still more. We are always chasing something. "Busy" keeps us moving so we don't have to look within. Forward movement is enough satisfaction for now. Our love of technology (especially computers) accelerates the speed of forward movement.

But I am a Christian who follows a nonviolent Jesus. Within that life, I can only give what I have. I had decided to stop "moving forward," for ten months, to stop being relevant to my culture, in an effort to be still and know that God is still God. I seek this experience of Divine Presence, an inner reassurance of the love of God, with bare-bones simplicity, an emptying out of anger, frustrations, and stress. While this process is happening, the fact exists that sitting atop this human frame is my conditioned mind, habitually afraid of doing nothing, of stilling the inner noise, allowing myself to become empty. Most of us fear the aching void within or are reluctant to look at ourselves, meet the person we might not like, who surely will be staring at us in our silence. I am convinced this fear of exposure keeps us from the effort to be still. Stillness and quiet are too intangible for our minds which always choose more. More is better. More is important. More is secure. But in the truly spiritual life, the still small voice is always "just enough."

THERAPEUTIC FASTING AND SLOWING DOWN

Creating this sabbatical environment had become a spiritual retreat wherein change of heart and mind leads to a change of daily routine. True change happens from the inside out. One powerful method that assists in altering our main inner landscapes is fasting. For the first three weeks of January, I engaged in a three-week cleansing diet followed by a three-day water fast. The cleansing diet consisted of limiting my eating to organic fruits and vegetables and drinking organic juice. The sabbatical was an attempt to let a changed person emerge from the old patterns of living. The old patterns include the daily assault of less than healthy food and drink. This most powerful of all asceticisms has tremendous therapeutic results of healing and rejuvenating body, mind, and soul. Without the subtle haze of too much eating, toxic food, and caffeine, I began to feel slower, more at peace, more centered and clear-headed. I slept more soundly, dreamed more deeply. I felt reborn. This was a good inner foundation for continuing my sabbatical journey.

HEADING FOR THE INNER LAND

Three months into our Sabbatical, Suzanne and I headed for separate retreats at the Jesuit-run Eastern Point Retreat House in Gloucester, Massachusetts for eight days of total silence, daily Mass and spiritual direction with one of the trained staff. With meals taken in silence, this self-contained solitude established a contemplative environment for us to discern the direction of our lives without the usual daily distractions.

My director encouraged us to reflect on the 25-year period Suzanne and I had spent helping to form and then living the Agape Community experience. Therefore, my first assignment from my spiritual director was to ponder all the ways I was utterly and completely grateful for 25 years at Agape. The list was lengthy. The more I reflected on the grace of it all, the more reasons surfaced for gratitude, a fortune of thankfulness. Suzanne, our daughter Teresa, and all the countless thousands of people and resources have made this life for me, (more or less), a joyous pleasure—superabundant, mindboggling, and challenging.

The next arena my director and I looked at was more daunting—the future. At age 60, the future means looking at the remaining (God-willing) one-quarter of my life. In our discussion, we began to establish a singular priority that would last for the remaining eight months of my sabbatical—the mystery of listening. If doing God's will is the basis of all fulfillment of our time on earth, then listening to that Divine whisper becomes the heart of the process. As the prophets spoke to their God: "Speak your servant is listening," then The Divine "speaking" to me remains one of the most exquisite of all mysteries, next to being alive at all.

My ego self is the voice I can usually hear, with the mind tirelessly analyzing, planning rehearsing, controlling. To listen to a speaking God at times requires a secluded place, a spiritually charged atmosphere to have any realistic chance at "hearing." The voice I heard began to define my sabbatical: "Slow down, disappear into the silence (goodbye to the ego noise) and listen."

The conversation with God, illuminated by the exchange with my spiritual director at Eastern Point, helped me to move outward to inward. "Contemplari" is what the Roman augers saw when they looked up to the sky into the sacred enclosure they called the "templum," related to the Greek word "theoria" or to look toward God. "Con" templation means looking toward this same God—within.

IN THE BELOVED COMMUNITY AT WESTON

After my retreat with the Jesuits, I headed to Weston, Vermont. The Benedictine monks gave us a cabin in their snow-covered meadow surrounded by great pines and mountains. Since the beginning of our sabbatical, I knew that I desired long periods of solitude, but only within the embrace of a Christian Community of prayer. A month-long retreat at Weston provided the solace of two worlds. First, the pastoral quiet of winter snowscapes provided comfort to the soul; and second, the experience of Weston was the fullest sense of the beloved community that I have experienced in a great while. I have always felt a freedom in this natural world, quiet where no volcanic insights come, just the same old yet reassuring "go slow, and trust." This spirit of retreat reminds me of the saying of Lao Tzu: "Who will prefer the jingle of jade pendants if one once has heard stone growing in a cliff?"[155]

One can't be within the Weston Priory Community long before love comes up, arriving like glowing candlelight, with the faces of the monks accenting the intoxicating cadences of the sweet love songs to God. Suzanne and I woke at 4:30 a.m. before the sun rose, for "lauds", and we spent each day within the rhythm of four daily prayer times, ending with Compline at 8 p.m.

Ninety percent of the prayers and liturgies consist of twelve monks singing, accompanied by the gathered faithful singing with them. I observed that the brothers love each other, love those that attend these liturgies, and the extended community reciprocates with great love for them. The author William Gass observes: "Because you are loved, you are now fuel for another's fire."[156] The poet Rainer Maria Rilke adds that "to be loved means to be consumed in the flames."[157] It seems that this month-long retreat at Weston accomplished learning and relearning something I've always known in the deeps—the whole point of the life in Christ, is to give and receive love. The daily prayer, meals in silence, the discussion with monks over the dishes, the conversation with the many extraordinary retreatants were just this—being consumed in this gentle and sweet conflagration. At month's end, it was hard to leave.

THE IMMENSE, UNTAMED GOD

Seven months into the Sabbatical, the time came for pilgrimage travel, which begins with leaving the familiar for the unfamiliar, moving from predictable routines to seeking God in the new and uncertain. I drove 2,500 miles from Massachusetts to Colorado to spend two months at Nada Hermitage with community members from the Spiritual Life Institute, friends whom I had known for 25 years.

Driving from Pennsylvania on, I began to encounter a sense of vast limitless space. By the time I crossed the Mississippi and preceded to Colorado, rural quickly replaced urban. Except for St. Louis, Kansas City, and Topeka, I saw almost limitless, uninhabited landscape. The flatlands of Kansas gave way to the sudden, dramatic 14,000 foot Rockies. These mountains revealed the massive display of the untamed God. Throughout my entire stay in Colorado, I felt this gnawing, pervasive sense of immensity. What could be more ancient, I thought, more immovable, more impervious to the human imprint and folly than these mountain ranges? Limitless size and space were my companions for two months, both overwhelming, and oddly reassuring.

I arrived at Nada Hermitage after a breathtaking four-hour car ride through the most beautiful of the southern Rockies. I easily settled into my hermitage, Juliana, in a community of six other retreatants and three community members with whom I began my two month stay. Most of my daily hermitage routine was solitary—up at 6 a.m. for morning meditation. I also participated in communal prayers and liturgy at midday, ending with 5 p.m. Vespers—three days a week. Sunday Mass was open to the public, followed by a brunch and lively conversation. Except for an hour here or an hour there, these two months were solitary. I spent a month alone, with Suzanne joining me for a month of a similar schedule.

Our hermitage community was located in Crestone, nestled in a flat desert valley, surrounded by the Sangre de Cristo Mountains of Southern Colorado, where I was immersed in what is called "desert spirituality," the path of sparse, stripped-down simplicity. The landscape sets the tone—desert for miles right outside my window. Sounds are exceedingly infrequent; wind during the day, coyotes howling at night. As the native people, who considered the specific land I was standing on sacred would say: "This land is so remote, so sacred, that only the wind could make a home here."

The solitude at the hermitage was a place apart and thankfully, almost completely void of our 21st Century sights and sounds. For two months, I experienced a sweetness in the somewhat barren, dry desert. Silence has always attracted me, and these two months in the quiet, taught me why. In a meditative environment, silence yields to a sense of peace, and this peace is still and undriven, and an undriven peace moves slowly; slow is quieting and yields to an even deeper stillness, which brings me into a sense of the serene. To experience this serenity is to feel the goodness of life, and to feel this goodness, empties out somewhat, the burning frustrations of life. I feel less the heat of this inner turmoil, and am my truer self before God. Being my more true self before God makes God more available and more known. So I continue to seek the Divine in this silence. The Trappists call it the "sweetness of God." We humans like sweet, as it represents God's reassuring goodness. Alone in silence, I was reminded of the words of St. John of the Cross: "Your fragrant breathing stills me."

To trade Agape's incessant demands for this solitude deeply satisfied my inner need for the true rest and a change. I intensified this solitude by leaving the hermitage community and traveling another 1,000 feet up the mountain to 9,000 feet and stayed four days in St. John of the Cross Hermitage. Although somewhat weakened by the lessening of oxygen, I was greeted by the most visually ecstatic moments of my entire sabbatical. Words would fail to describe this mountain view overlooking out over the valley. Again, no music, no radio, no other people, no other sound, except the wind and a vigorous stream flowing audibly next to my hermitage. I drank daily from this stream and bathed in its primitive and frigid purity.

The demands of Agape that I had left at home had always seemed like urgent ones—the painful state of the world, combined with the work that needs to be done, and done today. By contrast, in this solitude, I am before God, totally alone in the natural world—no breaking in from other humans. No one even knows where I am (except the Nada Community members down in the valley). The life of the natural world has its friendly interruptions, mostly hawks hovering and dramatic changes throughout the vast summer sky.

True solitude is the work of restoration which, almost everyone I know yearns for. But it is so much more. This more contemplative perch attunes me first to listening to myself and what I can continue to learn. In addition to the unusual gift of wilderness, solitude also attunes me, undistracted, to nature herself and the way nature lives around me.

The power of John Muir's journals and Thoreau's *Walden* is that in their actual writing process, their wisdom flowed from being totally alone in the natural world. Thoreau chose human-centered metaphors to grasp at the mystical nature of the untrammeled natural world around him. Muir wrote that he simply wanted others to fall in love with nature's loveliness. What could be more urgent for me than to feel nature's loveliness, given that I am often immersed in a society of human excess, living within the ever present image of a damaged environment caused by a world gone wrong? But even more intensely felt is the pure mystique of solitude. This mystery of being utterly alone always ends in a paradox. In being alone, I share this aloneness with everything around me, everything that is. In this wilderness solitude, I grow closer to the core of who I really am, more successfully than in much of human encounter. Philosopher John Cowper Powys cuts to the heart of this silence: "Only when the soul is alone can the magic of the universe flow through it. Our soul needs the silence for the murmurs of the long centuries to grow audible, for the mystery of the cosmic procession to make it felt."[158] Being "alone" is a glimpse of how my life really is.

IONA, SACRED PLACE AND THE FINAL PILGRIMAGE

Fr. Colman McGrath, a Scottish priest in residence at Iona, gave a homily at St. Michael's Chapel at the Abbey of Iona: "Always remember that you are in a very sacred place, where people have sacrificed to make a pilgrimage here for the past 1,500 years, trusting that they would find healing, reconciliation and love. The Isle of Iona, off the west coast of Scotland was a propitious place indeed to end our sabbatical. This island is made famous by St. Columba, a monk of the 6th Century who started a war over a holy book, then repented this sin of war-making by following his call to repentance. Columba left his beloved Ireland, finally establishing a community on Iona, still thriving after all these centuries. The Abbey of Iona is a community dedicated to nonviolent peace and works to abolish nuclear weapons and is a peace witness in the name of God. To deepen this ministry, the community gathers for prayer three times a day with pilgrims from all over the world.

So, as we completed our sabbatical by making this pilgrimage to Iona, Suzanne and I begged forgiveness for our wars in Iraq and Afghanistan, and like Columba, we sought to repent. For what? The ongoing sin of U.S. lifestyle that makes for war and a church that says nothing about that war. With that tall order, we still left Iona feeling cleansed and blessed, filled and restored by this beloved community, and ready to be called back to the beloved community at Agape.

Endnotes

Chapter 1

1 James Fowler, *Becoming Adult, Becoming Christian*, 70.

2 Leo Tolstoy, *Calendar of Wisdom*, 377.

3 Peter Maurin, "Aims and Means" (New York: Catholic Worker Newspaper, May 2005).

Chapter 2

4 Catherine Doherty, *Gospel Without Compromise* 49.

5 Catherine Doherty, "Apostolic Farming," Combermere ONT 46.

6 Henry David Thoreau, *Walden*, 105.

7 Wendell Berry, *Gift Of Good Land*, 113.

8 Alfred Delp, *Advent of the Heart, Seasonal Sermons and Prison Writings*, 149.

9 Raymond Bernano Blakeney, *Meister Eckhart, a Modern Translation*, 243.

10 Adrian House, *Francis of Assisi, a Revolutionary Life*, 94.

11 Adolf Holl, *The Last Christian*, 3.

12 Ibid.

13 Adrian House, *Francis of Assisi, a Revolutionary Life*, 82.

Chapter 3

14 Fr Bernard Haring, *The Healing Power of Peace and Nonviolence*, 25–26.

15 Ibid. 44.

16 Ibid. 58, 51.

17 Ibid. 41.

18 Martin Luther King Jr., *A Testament of Hope, The Essential Writings of Martin Luther*

King Jr., 256.

19   Vernard Eller, *War and Peace*, 100.

20   Lanza del Vasto, *Warriors of Peace*, 12.

21   Martin Luther King Jr. "The Better Way" speech, from audiotape *We Shall Overcome* (Phoenix Entertainment and Talent, 1984).

22   George MacRae SJ, lecture on the Gospels, Boston College, July 1986.

Chapter 4

23   Martin Luther King Jr., *A Testament of Hope, The Essential Writings of Martin Luther King Jr.*, 256.

24   Norman Cousins, ed., *Profiles of Gandhi*, 96.

25   John L. McKenzie S.J., *Dictionary of the Bible*, 902.

26   Pope John Paul II, "Dives and Misericordia, on the Mercy of God" 26, 39.

27   Ronald Sider, *Christ and Violence*, 31.

28   John Yoder, "What Would You Do If?", 99.

29   Fr Bernard Haring, *The Healing Power of Peace and Nonviolence*, 45.

Chapter 5

30   "Cardinal Law Compares Sept. 11 Horror to Auschwitz", National Catholic Reporter (Nov 2001).

31   U.S. Conference of Catholic Bishops, "A Pastoral Message: Living With Faith and Hope After Sep 11" (Nov 14, 2001).

32   Thomas Merton ed., *Gandhi on Nonviolence*, 40.

33   Martin Luther King Jr., *Testament of Hope, The Essential Writings of Martin Luther King Jr.*, 509.

34   Juan Mateos, "The Message of Jesus". Sojourners Magazine (June 1977).

35   Professor Ward Thomas, A Presentation on the Just War. Holy Cross College, 2007.

36   Barack Obama, Nobel Peace Prize Acceptance Speech. Oslo, Norway (Dec 10, 2009).

37   Ibid.

38   Fr John McKenzie, *The Power and Wisdom*, 45.

39   Ronald Sider, "A Call for Evangelicals", Christian Century 753–57.

40   Jacques Ellul, *Violence* 97.

41   Juan Tamayo, "Flashback to 1998: Pope John Paul II Visits Cuba", Miami Herald.

42   Martin Luther King Jr., *Testament of Hope, The Essential Writings of Martin Luther King Jr.*, 243.

Chapter 6

43 Palden Gyatso, *Autobiography of a Tibetan Monk*, In the Forward by The Dalai Lama.

44 Catherine of Siena, *The Dialogue*, 25.

45 "The Killing Screens", Media and the Culture of Violence.Media Education Foundation, 1994.

46 Sogyal Rinpoche, *The Tibetan Book of the Living and Dying*, 56–59.

47 Fr. Lucas of St. Joseph, O.C.D., *The Secret of Sanctity of St. John of the Cross*, 11.

Chapter 7

48 Eva Hoffman, "Home as Concentration Camp", New York Times (Oct 17, 1999).

49 Dr. James Gilligan, *Violence, a National Epidemic*, 39.

50 Ibid. 184.

51 Ibid. 113.

52 Ibid. 185.

53 Thomas Gordon, *The Discipline That Works*, 113–36.

Chapter 8

54 Henry David Thoreau, *Walden*, 22.

55 Thomas Merton, *No Man Is an Island*, 260.

56 Abraham Heschel, *Sabbath*, 9.

57 Ibid. 76.

58 Ibid. 59.

59 Ibid.3.

Chapter 9

60 Thomas Merton, ed. *Gandhi on Nonviolence*, 26, 48.

61 Lanza del Vasto, *Warriors of Peace*, 48.

62 M.K. Gandhi, Statement in Court. March 23, 1922; Ahmadabad, India.

63 Thomas Merton, ed. *Gandhi on Nonviolence*, 34.

64 Walter Wink, *Engaging the Powers*, 206.

65 Ibid. 205.

66 Carl G. Jung, "After the Catastrophe", Civilization in Transition (1945).

67 Walter Wink, *Engaging the Powers*, 206.

68 Wendell Berry, *Collected Poems 1957–1982*, "Manifesto, The Mad Farmer Liberation Front," 152.

69   Thomas Merton, ed. *Gandhi on Nonviolence*, 48.

70   Richard Heinberg, *The Party's Over*, 211.

71   U.S. Government Spending (usgovernmentspending.com), Budget of U.S. Government 2011.

72   E.F. Schumacher, *Small is Beautiful*, 57.

73   Ibid. 58.

74   Ibid. 58–59.

75   Lanza del Vasto, *Warriors of Peace*, 48.

76   Ibid. 48.

77   Robert Thurman, *Inner Revolution*, 218.

78   M.K. Gandhi, *All Men Are Brothers*, 218.

79   M.K. Gandhi, *Nonviolence in Peace and War*, 216.

80   Poem by Daniel Berrigan sent to the author.

Chapter 10

81   usgovernmentspending.com

82   Walter Brueggemann, *The Prophetic Imagination*, 41.

83   Ibid. 41.

84   Gene Sharp, *The Politics of Nonviolent Action, Part I, Power and Struggle*, 19–21.

Chapter 11

85   Los Angeles Times; January 15, 2000.

86   Anup Shah, "Poverty Facts and Stats", Global Issues Update; September 20, 2010.

87   Cees Hamelink, Digital Advance. June 1, 1998.

88   "The Killing Screens", Media and the Culture of Violence.Media Education Foundation, 1994.

89   William F. Leuchtenburg, *Perils of Prosperity*, 200.

90   Ibid. 196.

91   Ibid. 242.

92   Federal Reserve Joint Economic Committee, Sallie Mae Trans Union. Jan 4, 2012.

93   Magna Global Advertising Forecast, "Steady Growth with Soft Underpinnings in 2011." Press Release Jan 18, 2011.

94   U.S. Food and Agriculture Association, "State of Food Insecurity", 2003.

95   BBC T.V. documentary, "A Dollar a Day". Nov 4, 2009.

96   Paul Krugman, "For Richer". New York Times; Oct 20, 2002. 65.

Chapter 12

97   Jacques Ellul, *Anarchy and Christianity*, 58.

98   Vernard Eller, *Christian Anarchy*, 6.

99   Ibid. XIII.

100   D.G. Tendulkar, *Mahatma: Life of Mohandas Karamchand Gandhi*, Vol.8 278–80.

101   Walter Wink, *Engaging the Powers*, 55.

102   Mahatma Gandhi, *All Men Are Brothers*, 127–28, 136.

Chapter 13

103   Leo Tolstoy, *Writings on Civil Disobedience and Nonviolence*, 297–302.

104   Dom Helder Camera, *Questions for Living*, 93–94.

105   Gutierrez's comment made in a course on Liberation Theology at Boston College, July 1984.

106   Jacques Ellul, *Violence: Reflecting from a Christian Perspective*, 100.

107   Richard Garfield, "Morbidity and Mortality Among Iraqi Children", casi.org.uk. July 1999.

108   Martin Luther King Jr., *A Testament of Hope, Essential Writings of Martin Luther King Jr.*, 249.

Chapter 14

109   Leo Tolstoy, *Civil Disobedience and Nonviolence* 102.

110   Ibid. 102.

111   Martin Luther King Jr., *A Testament of Hope, Essential Writings of Martin Luther King Jr.*, 207.

112   Jonathan Schell, "No More Unto the Breach," Harper's Magazine. March 2003, 23.

113   Michael Brower, Warren Leon, *The Consumer's Guide to Effective Environmental Choices*, 4.

114   Michael Ignatieff, "The Burden", New York Times Magazine. January 5, 2003. 23.

115   Ibid. 24.

116   W.H. Auden, *The Age of Anxiety*.

117   Martin Luther King Jr., *A Testament of Hope, Essential Writings of Martin Luther King Jr.*, 277.

118   Jonathan Schell, "No More Unto the Breach," Harper's Magazine. March 2003, 41.

119   Ibid. 41.

120   Thomas Merton, *Conjectures of a Guilty Bystander*, 117.

Chapter 15

121   Martin Luther Jr., *Strength to Love*, 42.

122   En.wikipedia.org/civiliancasualtiesinwarinafghanistan2001-present

123   Luke Mogelson, "Pacifists in the Crossfire," New York Times Magazine. May 20. 2012. 46.

124   Neil MacFarquhar, Huwaida Said, "Many Children Among Victims of Syrian Force," New York Times. May 27, 2012.

125   wikipedia.org/wiki/israelipalestinianconflict

Chapter 16

126   Leo Tolstoy, *The Raid and Other Stories*.

127   President Dwight D. Eisenhower, "Military Industrial Complex Speech", 1961.

128   Paul Roberts, *End of Oil*, 15.

129   ibid. 111.

130   Wayne Miller, *Sabbath*, 99,31.

131   Bill McKibben, *Deep Economy*, 114.

132   E.F. Schumacher, *Small Is Beautiful*, 33.

133   Rene Girard, *Violence and the Sacred*, 147.

134   ibid. 145–46.

135   ibid. 145.

136   E.F. Schumacher, *Good Work*, 1.

Chapter 17

137   Thomas Aquinas, *Summa Theologica*, Part I, Issue 2 256.

138   Claus Westermann, *Genesis. A Commentary*, 159.

139   "Orion", March/April 2005. 18,23.

Chapter 18

140   Sally McFague, *Supernatural Christians*, 12.

141   Steen, Steen, Bainbridge and Eisenberg, *The Straw Bale House*, 25.

142   ibid. 28.

143   Joseph Jenkins, *The Humanure Handbook*, 40.

144   US Department of Agriculture, updated 2011.

145   Richard Heinberg, *The Party's Over*, 195.

146   U.S. Environmental Protection Agency 2008, Inventory of Greenhouse Gas

Emissions and Sinks, 473.

147   Food and Agricultural Organization of UN , 2012 (website).

148   John Campbell, "Saving the Planet One Meal at a Time" Vol. 3. Issue 2, Fall 2007.

149   ibid.

150   John Robbins, "2500 Gallons All Wet", from earthsave.com.

151   Henry David Thoreau, *Walden*.

152   John A. McDougall, MD, *Digestive Tune Up*, 136–38.

153   Gidon Eshel, Pamela Martin, "New Scientist". Dec 17, 2005. 17.

154   Henry David Thoreau, *Walden*, 271.

Chapter 19

155   Lao Tzu,John C.H. Wu (Translator), *Tao Te Ching*, 1961

156   Philip Koch, *Solitude: A Philosophical Encounter*, 1994

157   Rilke, Rainer Maria, Magda Von Hattinberg (Editor), Joel Agee (Translator) *Rilke and Benvenuta: an Intimate Correspondence.*

158   John Cowper Powys, *A Philosophy of Solitude*, 1933

Bibliography

Aquinas, Saint Thomas, "The "Summa Theologica" Part 1, Issue 2." R. & T. Washbourne, ltd., 1912

Arberry, A.J. translated. "The Koran, Interpreted" New York, Collier Books, 1955.

Auden, W.H. "The Age of Anxiety" Buccaneer Books. 1994.

BBC T.V. Documentary, "A Dollar a Day" Nov 4, 2009.

Berry, Wendell. "Collected Poems 1957–1982" San Francisco, North Point Press. 1984.

Bower, Michael; Leon, Warren."The Consumer's Guide to Effective Environmental Choices" New York, Three Rivers Press. 1999.

Brueggemann, Walter. "The Prophetic Imagination" USA Fortress Press. 1978.

Camara, Dom Helder. "Questions for Living" Orbis Books; Revised edition edition.Jun 27 2002

Campbell, John. "Saving Planet One Meal at a Time." Peace Power—Berkeley's Journal of Nonviolence & Conflict Transformation Vol. 3, Issue 2, Fall 2007.

en.wikipedia.org/civiliancasultiesinwarinafghanistan 2001-present

Cousins, Norman, Ed. "Profiles of Gandhi" Delhi, India Book Co. 1969.

del Vasto, Lanza. "Warriors of Peace" New York, Alfred A. Knopf. 1974.

Delp, Alfred S. J. "Advent of the Heart: Seasonal Sermons and Prison Writings, 1941- 44" San Francisco, Ignatius Press. 2006.

Doherty, Catherine, "Apostolic Farming". Combermere Ont. Canada, Madonna House Publications.

Eckhart, Meister. "Meister Eckhart, A Modern Translation" New York, Harper Collins Publishers. 1941.

Eisenhower, President Dwight D. "Military Industrial Complex Speech." 1961.

Eller, Vernard."Christian Anarchy: Jesus' Primacy over the Powers" Grand Rapids, Michigan, William B. Eerdmans Publishing Co. 1987.

Ellul, Jacques. "Anarchy and Christianity" Eugene, Oregon, Wipf and Stock Publishers. 1988.

Gandhi, Mohandas K. "All Men Are Brothers" New York, Continuum Publishing Corp. 1982.

Gandhi, Mohandas K. "Nonviolence in Peace and War" Housmans Bookshop; New Ed Edition. December 1962.

Ellul, Jacques. "Violence: Reflections from a Christian Perspective" New York, The Seabury Press. 1969.

Eshel, Gidon; Martin, Pamela."New Scientist Magazine". December 17, 2005.

Bibliography

Federal Reserve Joint Economic Committee, Sallie Mae Trans Union. January 4, 2012.

Food and Agriculture Organization of the UN. 2012. (website)

Fowler, James. "Becoming Adult Becoming Christian, Adult Development and Christian Faith" San Francisco, Harper and Row. 1984.

Gandhi, Mohandas. "Statement in Court", Ahmedabad, India. March 23, 1922.

Garfield, Richard. "Morbidity and Mortality Among Iraqi Children." casi.org.uk, July 1999.

Gerbner, George, "The Killing Screens, Media and a Culture of Violence." Media Education Foundation, 1994.

Gilligan, James, M.D. "Violence: Reflections on a National Epidemic" New York, Vintage Books. 1997.

Girard, Rene. Gregory, Patrick (Translator) "Violence and the Sacred" Baltimore, The Johns Hopkins University Press. 1972.

Gordon, Thomas. "Discipline that Works: Promoting Self-Discipline in Children" New York, A Plume Book. 1989.

Gutierrez, Gustavo. Comment made in a course on liberation theology at Boston College. July 1984.

Gyatso, Palden; Tsering Shakya, Translator "The Autobiography of a Tibetan Monk" New York, Grove Press. 1997.

Hamelink, Cees. Digital Advance. June 1, 1998.

Haring, Bernhard. "The Healing Power of Peace and Nonviolence" New York, Paulist Press. 1980.

Heinberg, Richard. "The Party's Over: Oil, War and the Fate of Industrial Societies" Gabriola Island, BC, Canada, New Society Publishers. 2003.

Heschel, Abraham. "The Sabbath" Boston, Shambhala Publications. 2003.

Hoffman, Eva. "Home as Concentration Camp."New York Times. Oct 17, 1999.

Holl, Adolph. "The Last Christian." Garden City, N.J., Doubleday and Co. 1980.

House, Adrian. "Francis of Assisi, a Revolutionary Life" Mahwah, New Jersey, Paulist Press. 2001.

Ignatieff, Michael. "The Burden." New York Times Magazine. January 5, 2003. Wikipedia. org/wiki/israelipalestinianconflict

Jenkins, Joseph. "The Humanure Handbook: A Guide to Composting Human Manure" White River Junction, Vermont, Chelsea Green Publishing Co., 1999.

Jung, Carl G. Civilization in Transition "After the Catastrophe." 1945.

King Jr., Martin Luther. "A Testament of Hope, the Essential Writings and Speeches of Martin Luther King Jr." Ed., James M. Washington. San Francisco, Harper and Row Publishers. 1986.

King Jr., Martin Luther. "Strength to Love." New York, Harper and Row. 1963.

Krugman, Paul. "For Richer" New York Times, Oct 20, 2002.

Law, Cardinal Bernard. "Cardinal Law compares Sept. 11 horror to Auschwitz." National Catholic Reporter. November 2001.

Leuchtenburg, William E. "The Perils of Prosperity: 1914–1932." Chicago, University of Chicago Press. 1958.

Los Angeles Times, January 2000.

MacFarquhar, Neil; Said, Huwaida. "Many Children Among Victims of Syrian Attack." N.Y. Times, May 27th 2012.

MacRae, George, SJ. "Lecture on Gospel of John." Boston College, 1984.

Magna Global Advertising Forecast, "Steady Growth with Soft Underpinnings in 2011" Press Release Jan 18, 2011.

Mateos, Juan. "The Message of Jesus" Sojourners Magazine, Washington, DC. June 1977.

McDougall, MD, John A. "Digestive Tune-Up" Summertown Tennessee, Healthy Living Publications. 2006.

McFague, Sally. "Super, Natural Christians: How We Should Love Nature" Minneapolis, Fortress Press. 1997.

McKenzie, Fr John. "Dictionary of the Bible" New York, MacMillan Publishing Co. 1965.

McKibben, Bill. "Deep Economy: The Wealth of Communities and the Durable Future" New York, Henry Holt and Co. 2007.

Merton, Thomas. "Conjectures of a Guilty Bystander" New York, Image Books. 1965.

Merton, Thomas Ed. "Gandhi on Nonviolence: A Selection From the Writings of Mahatma Gandhi" New York, New Directions Publishing Co. 1964.

Merton, Thomas. "No Man is an Island" New York, Harcourt Brace. 1955.

Mogelson, Luke. "Pacifists in the Crossfire."N.Y. Times. May 20, 2012.

Muller, Wayne. "Sabbath: Finding Rest, Renewal, and Delight in Our Busy Lives" New York, Bantam Books, 1999.

Obama, Barack. Nobel Peace Prize Acceptance Speech. Oslo, Norway. Dec 10, 2009.

Orion, March/April 2005.

Pope John Paul II, "Dives in Misericordia, On the Mercy of God."

Rinpoche, Sogyal. "The Tibetan Book of Living and Dying" New York, Harper San Francisco. 1994.

Roberts, Paul. "The End of Oil: On the Edge of a Perilous New World" Boston, Houghton Mifflin Co. 2004.

Robbins, John. "2500 Gallons All Wet" from earthsave.com

Schell, Jonathan. "No More Unto the Breach." Harper's Magazine. March 2003.

Schumacher, E.F. "Good Work" New York, Harper and Row Publishers. 1979.

Schumacher, E.F. "Small is Beautiful: Economics as if People Mattered" London, Harper and Row Publishers. 1973.

Shah, Anup."Poverty Facts and Stats."Global Issues Update. September 20, 2010.

Sharp, Gene. "The Politics of Nonviolent Action.Part I, Power and Struggle" Boston, Porter Sargent Publishers. 1973.

Sider, Ronald J. "Christ and Violence" Scottdale Pa., Herald Press. 1979.

Sider, Ronald J. "An Evangelical Call To Civic Responsibility: Ron Sider's comments at the launch of the NAE's new document" March 2012

Siena, Catherine of. "Catherine of Siena: The Dialogue" Paulist Press. April 1980.

St. Joseph, Fr. Lucas of. "The Secret of Sanctity of St. John of the Cross" Bruce; First Edition edition. 1962.

Steen, Steen, Bainbridge, Eisenberg. "The Straw Bale House" White River Junction, Vermont, Chelsea Green Publishing Co. 1994.

Tamayo, Juan. "Flashback to 1998: Pope John Paul II Visits Cuba." Miami Herald, 1998.

Tendulkar, D.G. "Mahatma: Life of Mohandas Karamchand Gandhi, Vol 1, 1869- 1920" Ministry of Information and Broadcasting

"The Arms and Means of the Catholic Worker."New York Catholic Worker Newspaper, 2005.

"The Killing Screens, Media and the Culture of Violence."Media Education Foundation, 1994.

Bibliography

Thoreau, Henry David. "Walden, Life in the Woods" Ticknor and Fields: Boston Original Publisher. 1854

Thurman, Robert. "Inner Revolution: Life, Liberty, and the Pursuit of Real Happiness" New York, Riverhead Books. 1998.

Tolstoy, Leo. "A Calendar of Wisdom: Daily Thoughts to Nourish the Soul" New York, Scribner. 1997.

Tolstoy, Leo. Louise and Aylmer Maude, Translator "Leo Tolstoy: The Raid and Other Stories" Oxford University Press, USA June 24, 1999.

Tolstoy, Leo. "Writings on Civil Disobedience and Nonviolence" New York, Bergman Publishers. 1967.

U.S. Conference of Catholic Bishops, "A Pastoral Message: Living with Faith and Hope After September 11". November 14, 2001.

U.S. Department of Agriculture, updated 2011.

U.S. Environmental Protection Agency "Inventory of Greenhouse Gas Emissions and Sinks" 2008.

U.S. Food and Agriculture Association, "State of Food Insecurity." 2003.

usgovernmentspending.com

U.S. Government Spending (usgovernmentspending.com), Budget of U.S. Government 2011.

Ward, Thomas. "A Presentation on the Just War Theory" Holy Cross College. 2007.

Westermann, Claus. "Genesis 1–11: A Continental Commentary" Fortress Press; 1st Fortress Press ed edition January 5, 1994

Wink, Walter. "Engaging the Powers: Discernment and Resistance In a World of Domination" Minneapolis, Fortris Press. 1992.

Yoder, John. "What Would You Do If?" Journal of Religious Ethics. 1974.